# My First History of Canada

by
## Donalda Dickie
with Illustrations by
Lloyd Scott

Revised and Updated by Rudiger Krause
**Red Leaf Press**

Originally published in 1958 as "My First History of Canada"

by Donalda Dickie, J.M. Dent & Sons (Canada) Limited, Vancouver
with Illustrations by Lloyd Scott

Permission to reprint the text granted by the Estate of Donalda J.Dickie

Permission to reprint the illustrations granted by Orion House (Britain)

This book is copyright. It may not be reproduced whole or in part by any method without permission in writing from the publisher.

ISBN 0-9681023-1-X
1996, 1997, 1999, 2002, 2005

Printed and bound in Canada
by Friesens Corporation, Manitoba

Published by Red Leaf Press
A Division of WT Educational Services
Telephone 604 264 1199

# ORIGINAL FOREWORD ("Foreword for Girls and Boys") by Donalda Dickie

This is a book that has many stories in it, and there is something special about each one of them: each story is about Canada. The stories are told in order; the ones that happened a long time ago are told at the beginning of the book, the ones that have only just happened are told at the end of the book. All the separate little stories, put down one after the other, tell one big, important story. That story is the story of Canada, we call it the *history* of Canada.

Can you find Canada on the map? In this book you will read that the people at the beginning of our history had never heard of our country, and did not know where it was. You will read how those people found Canada. Then you will read how other people journeyed from Canada's east coast all the way to her west coast. Later, you will find out how Canadians learned to govern themselves and how they have learned and are still learning to use Canada's many riches, such as her farm land, her forests, and her minerals.

Canada's story does not end with the last chapter in this book. Her story is still going on, and, of course, there are people in the story today, just as there always have been. You and I are some of the people in today's story! When we read a tale of adventure, we begin at the beginning of it, and then read on to see what exciting thing happened next. By doing that, we know how and why the adventure took place. The story of Canada is an adventure story, and *My First History of Canada* will tell you what happened in the story before you and I joined in.

# FOREWORD TO THIS ADAPTATION

Many histories of Canada have been written over the years, for adults and for children. Some of the best of these were penned by Donalda Dickie between the 1920's and the 1950's. Her stories make history come alive. She understood the purpose and destiny of Canada's story. She was able to write about the accomplishments as well as the mistakes of the past. Always her stories were written with the express purpose of making the young readers better citizens and informed participants in the ongoing story of our country.

It is unfortunate that her writings are all but forgotten. With this book we are making available to this generation of young Canadians one of the treasures of our past. Donalda Dickie deserves to be remembered; her contribution to the education of Canadians has been invaluable.

On the whole only minor changes have been made to the text. Some of these were stylistic; others corrected historical errors. We must remember that Miss Dickie wrote this history before the Viking village on the north coast of Newfoundland was uncovered, and, speaking of Newfoundland, just shortly after this tenth province had joined Canada.

However, a whole new chapter was written to bring Canada's story up to the present. And there are, here and there, additions to the original text, for instance, the section on the invention of the Cree alphabet.

# QUESTIONS and ACTIVITIES

At the end of the book there are Questions and Activities for each chapter. Some of these were included in the original edition; others have been written for this new one. They can help you learn more about Canada's story.

Some of the questions are meant for you to think about *before* you read the chapter; they should get you thinking and wondering, even if you don't know the answers yet. You may also answer them orally or in writing *after* you have done your reading.

The other Questions and Activities are there for you to do some thinking, exploring and creating after you have read the chapter. Maybe you can think of other things to do and other questions to research. Perhaps you will be interested enough to read other books on Canada's past. But don't think that you have to do all the questions and activities; just choose the ones that interest you the most.

If you do want to do some reading, writing and drawing we recommend that you get a binder or folder to keep everything together. Then at the end of the book you can look back at all the work you have done.

Of course, the Questions and Activities may be ignored completely if you just want to read the story.

Okanagan Centre, 1996

# CONTENTS

**1 The People in the Story**
1. The Indians were the first Canadians. 1
2. Glooscap: an Indian hero. 4
3. The white men came from Europe. 5

**2 How America Was Discovered Again (1400-1500)**
1. Some people thought that the earth was a globe. 7
2. Christopher Columbus discovered America in 1492. 9
3. John Cabot discovered Canada in 1497. 11

**3 How White Men Came to Live in Canada (1500-1600)**
1. French fishermen found the way in. 14
2. Jacques Cartier's men traded buttons for furs and drank down a spruce tree in 1534. 16
3. Sir Humphrey Gilbert took Newfoundland for England in 1583. 18
4. Sir Francis Drake took the west coast for England in 1579. 20

**4 At First Canada Was All French (1600-1612)**
1. Champlain reported on Canada. 23
2. De Monts built Port Royal in 1605. 24
3. Champlain built Quebec and fought the Iroquois. 25
4. John Guy built Cupids and picnicked with the Beothuks in 1610. 28
5. Henry Hudson discovered Hudson Bay in 1610. 30

**5 The Settlers Worked Hard to Get a Start (1610-1642)**
1. Champlain laid out the fur trade trail to the west. 32
2. The English took Acadia, but the French took her back. 34
3. Quebec had the first church and school. 35
4. Father Jogues was a hero. 36

**6 Both English and French Colonies Had to Fight for Their Lives (1612-1660)**
1. The Newfoundlanders fought the pirates. 38

|   |   |   |
|---|---|---|
|   | 2. The Acadians fought each other. | 38 |
|   | 3. Good women built a school and a hospital at Quebec. | 39 |
|   | 4. Ville Marie, the City of Mary. | 41 |
|   | 5. The Iroquois killed the Hurons. | 42 |
|   | 6. The heroes saved Canada. | 43 |
| 7 | **Canada Began to Grow (1658-1672)** |   |
|   | 1. Radisson and Groseilliers saved Canada's trade. | 46 |
|   | 2. Radisson and Groseilliers led the English to Hudson Bay. | 48 |
|   | 3. Talon set Canada on her feet. | 50 |
|   | 4. The good coureurs worked for Canada. | 52 |
|   | 5. The Newfoundlanders fought the fishing admirals. | 53 |
|   | 6. Newcomers in Newfoundland. | 54 |
| 8 | **Canada Spread North, West, and South (1670-1690)** |   |
|   | 1. Talon took possession of the north and west. | 55 |
|   | 2. Jolliet explored the Mississippi River in 1673. | 56 |
|   | 3. Governor Frontenac made the Iroquois behave. | 58 |
|   | 4. La Salle took the south-west for Canada in 1682. | 59 |
|   | 5. The boy Kelsey discovered the prairies in 1690. | 61 |
| 9 | **The French Canadians Fought the Iroquois and the English for Canada (1660-1700)** |   |
|   | 1. The fight for Hudson Bay. | 64 |
|   | 2. The wasp's nest. | 66 |
|   | 3. The English won in Acadia in 1690. | 68 |
|   | 4. Frontenac saved Quebec for France. | 69 |
|   | 5. The story of Madeleine of Vercheres | 71 |
| 10 | **Peace and War: Good Times and Hard Times (1700-1760)** |   |
|   | 1. The Canadians enjoyed themselves. | 74 |
|   | 2. The Verendryes led Canada out across the prairies. | 76 |
|   | 3. The Newfoundlanders got a Governor. | 78 |
|   | 4. The English built Halifax. | 80 |
|   | 5. Governor Lawrence exiled the Acadians. | 81 |
|   | 6. How the British won Canada. | 82 |

11 **The French and the English Got On Well Together (1763-1795)**
   1. In Quebec they helped each other.   86
   2. The Governor called the Acadians home.   87
   3. French and British Canadians became partners in the fur trade.   89
   4. English sailors explored Canada's west coast.   92

12 **The United Empire Loyalists Came to Canada (1775-1840)**
   1. The English colonies became the United States.   96
   2. The Loyalists went to Nova Scotia and Prince Edward Island, and made the new province of New Brunswick.   97
   3. Governor Haldimand helped the Loyalists in Quebec.   99
   4. The Loyalists started Ontario.   100
   5. The Canadians began to govern themselves.   101

13 **The Canadians Won the Relay Race to the Pacific Ocean (1750-1810)**
   1. Anthony Henday carried the baton to Alberta.   104
   2. Peter Pond led the Canadians into Athabaska.   107
   3. Alexander Mackenzie won the great relay race.   109
   4. Simon Fraser won the race for the Fraser River country.   112
   5. David Thompson lost the race for the Columbia.   113

14 **Red River Was the First Settlement in Western Canada (1811-1866)**
   1. The Silver Chief started the Red River settlement.   116
   2. The Nor'Westers tried to destroy Red River.   117
   3. The two companies united as the Hudson's Bay Company.   119
   4. Governor George Simpson was young and merry.   120
   5. Enter British Columbia.   122

15 **The Pioneers (1815-1850)**
   1. Next came the pioneers: they worked hard.   124
   2. The pioneers had fun too.   126
   3. The pioneers were great builders.   128
   4. Canada got two new kinds of business.   130

**16 Bringing In the Prairies (1850-1885)**
  1. The people of the great plains. 134
     The Indians hunt the buffalo
     The bad men
  2. Canada sent the North West Mounted Police
     to keep order. 136
     Prairie Chicken Old Man
     The Sitting Bull story
  3. The Canadians built the Canadian Pacific Railway
     to tie the provinces together. 140

**17 The Provinces United to Make Our Canada (1850-1885)**
  1. The provinces were growing up. 144
  2. The provinces all built schools and colleges. 146
  3. The Assemblies made the Governors and Councils
     do what the people wanted. 148
  4. Four of the provinces united to form the
     Dominion of Canada. 149
  5. Red River made her choice. 151
  6. The Metis rebellion. 155
  7. Gold! Gold on the Fraser! 157

**18 The Eastern Provinces Went Into New Industries (1850-1895)**
  1. Nova Scotia went into coal and steel. 161
  2. Quebec led the way in mining. 163
  3. New Brunswick made new uses of her timber. 164
  4. Prince Edward Island invented fox farming. 166
  5. Newfoundland found an iron mine and built a railway. 167
  6. Ontario had the first oil wells in Canada. 168

**19 The West Got New People (1870-1905)**
  1. First came the cowboys. 169
  2. The homesteaders. 172
  3. Missionaries gave the Indians a written language. 174
  4. New Canadians came from Europe. 175
     The Mennonites
     The Icelanders

The Doukhobors
5. Wheat made Canada world famous. 178
6. People kept on coming to Canada. 180
7. Alberta and Saskatchewan became provinces. 181

## 20 Canada in Three Wars (1900-1950)
1. Canadians helped Britain in the Boer War. 183
2. After the First World War Canada became a nation. 183
3. Then came the boom. 186
4. The bush pilots opened up the great northland. 187
5. When the boom burst. 188
6. The Second World War. 190
7. The years after the war brought many new Canadians. 193
8. Newfoundland joined Canada. 194

## 21 Bringing Canada's Story Up to the Present (1950 to now)
1. A mari usque ad mare. 196
2. Canada belongs to two big societies. 199
   The Commonwealth
   The United Nations
3. Canada gets a flag and an anthem. 201
4. Canada has a big birthday party. 202
5. Canada develops her natural and human resources. 202
6. Problems and opportunities. 203

**Questions and Activities** 205

**Index** 225

# 1  The People in the Story

## 1. The Indians were the first Canadians

For a long time there were no people in Canada; only animals lived here. There were huge dinosaurs, fierce bears, wolves, musk oxen, deer, and many small animals. At last the Indians and Inuit found Canada. They came from Asia. Probably they crossed over at the north-west corner where Asia and America almost touch each other. Perhaps they were hunting and followed the animals they were chasing across the ice.

These first Canadians were hunters and fishermen. They did not farm or live in towns, but moved round the country after the animals they were hunting. The wide spaces of Canada were good hunting grounds. More and more Indians came over till they spread all over Canada and the rest of America.

Several families of Indians lived together in a band; they hunted together and shared their food with one another. When they found a good place to hunt, they camped. The people in each family built a hut out of whatever they could find in their hunting grounds. The different materials they used - logs, hides, bark or ice - gave their buildings different shapes. They are called wigwams, long houses, teepees, or igloos.

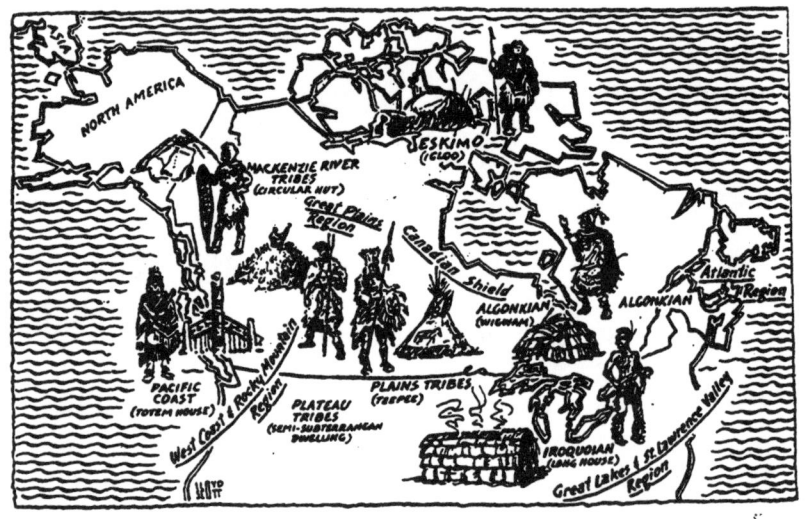

These Indians and Inuit were good hunters and trappers. They slipped through the woods as silently as shadows. They set traps for the animals, or shot them with bows and arrows. The arrows had heads made of flint, a kind of stone. All over Canada people used to find these flint arrow heads. Now you may see them in museums.

The Indians used every part of the animals they killed. They ate the meat and made clothes of the fur and the skins. They used the skins also to cover their teepees and wigwams and make moccasins. They twisted the sinews of the animals into strings for their bows, and the women used them for thread. Out of the bones, horns, teeth, and claws of the animals they made needles, knives, cups, bowls, and jewellery.

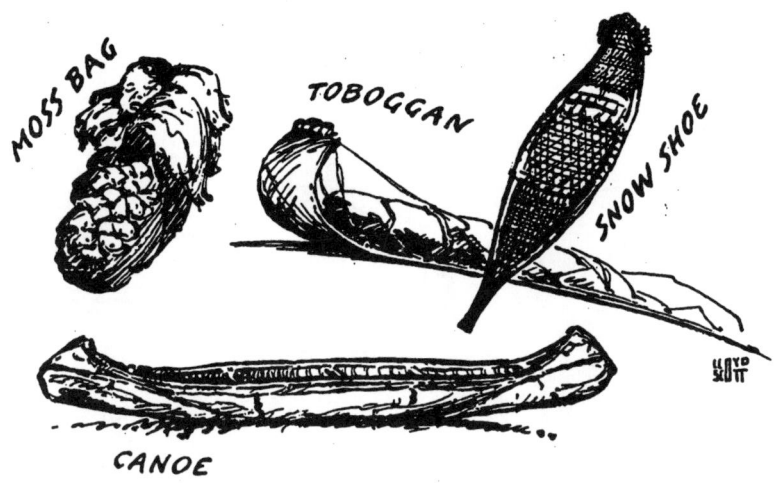

In summer the Indians travelled in canoes. In winter they went on snowshoes, hauling their things on toboggans. The women carried their babies on their backs in mossbags. They made the mossbags by wrapping the baby in moss and laying him on a board which they had placed on a skin. Then they folded the skin over and laced it up the front so that only the head of the papoose showed.

All the Indian bands which spoke the same language made up a tribe. Some of the tribes had similar languages. For example, the Micmac, Huron, Ojibwa, Cree & Blackfoot Indians were all part of the Algonkian tribes which stretched from the Atlantic Ocean to the Rockies. Other large tribal groups were the Inuit and the Athapaskan. There were also some smaller tribes, mainly between the Rockies and the Pacific Ocean. You can read their names on the map.

Each tribe had its own chiefs and its own hunting grounds. Every summer all the bands of a tribe gathered together for two or three weeks of feasting and dancing. At this meeting the tribe chose its chiefs. Then the chief and the medicine men held a council meeting. They made long speeches and made plans for peace or for war.

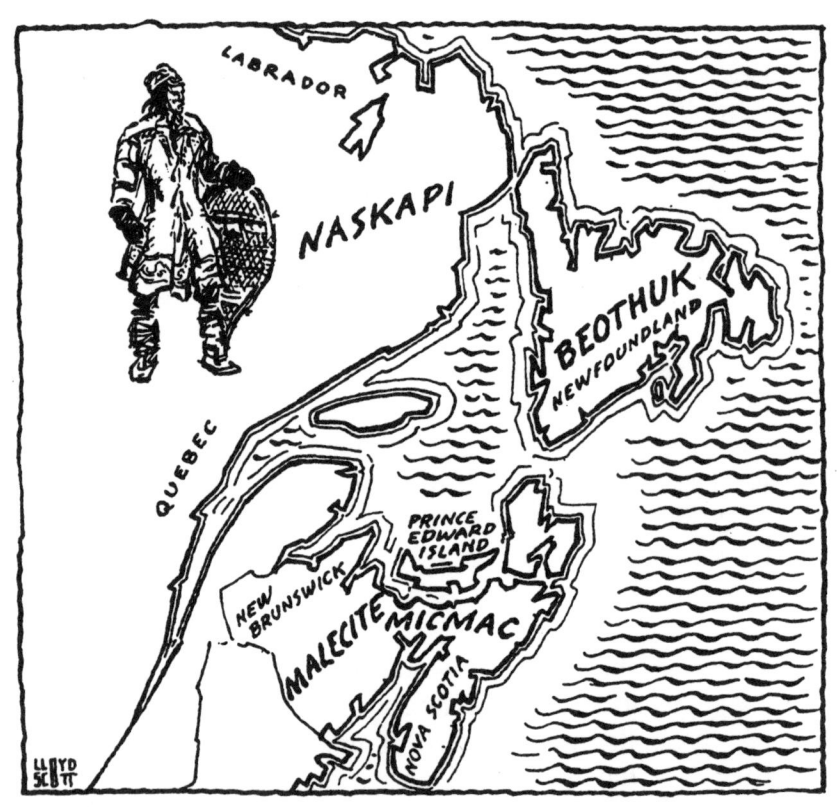

## 2. Glooscap: an Indian hero

The Indians and Inuit did not read or write; but they were great story tellers. Each tribe had many stories and songs. In the evening the old men told the stories of their tribe to the children. A Micmac story tells how their god or hero, Glooscap, brought summer to Canada.

The old men said that in the very long ago it was always cold in Canada. Then Glooscap and his grandmother came to live there. They built a wigwam near the mouth of the Big River. The grandmother did not like the snow and ice and cold winds, so Glooscap went to complain about them to Giant Winter. The Giant invited Glooscap into his great, glittering ice-wigwam, and they sat down to smoke. While they smoked, Winter put Glooscap to sleep for six months. When he woke, Glooscap hurried off south with steps a mile long. At each step the air grew warmer and more leaves and flowers came out. Soon Glooscap met Queen Summer. She wore a crown of flowers and was dancing with her children. Glooscap snatched her up and carried her home to his grandmother. The old lady was kind to Queen Summer and she stayed with them for six months. Ever since then, the old men say, Canada has had six months spring and summer, and six months fall and winter.

**3. The white men came from Europe.**

In about 1000, young Biarni of Iceland sailed for Greenland to spend Christmas with his friends there. A storm came up and blew his little ship past Greenland to a land that no white man had ever seen before. The shore was covered with trees. There are few trees in Greenland, so Biarni knew that he had gone too far. He turned round and sailed back to Greenland.

At the Christmas party, Biarni told his friends about the Land of Trees. Leif Ericsson, the son of Eric the Red who had come from Norway to live in Greenland, was young and brave. The Greenlanders needed wood, so Leif bought Biarni's ship and sailed away in the spring to find this new Land of Trees and to get wood for his people.

Leif and his men were the first white people ever to set foot in our country.

The Greenlanders thought it very beautiful. The trees were tall and the open spaces were covered with grass, flowers, and grape-vines. There were so many grape-vines that Leif named the new country Vineland.

The Greenlanders stayed in Vineland all that winter, working hard every day. Some cut down trees and stripped off the branches. Others hauled the logs to the shore and loaded them onto the ship. By spring they had their ship full of wood and wine, and they sailed proudly home to Greenland.

After that Leif's brother, his sister, and several of their friends made trips to the new land. They built a village here, but the Indians killed so many of them that the others gave it up and sailed home.

The Greenlanders never returned to Vineland, but they told their children and grandchildren about the beautiful Land of Trees beyond the western sea. They made songs and stories about it. By and by they forgot that it was a real land; they thought it was just a story - a legend.

# 2

# How America Was Discovered Again
## 1400 to 1500

**1. Some people thought that the earth was a globe.**

By this time the people in Asia, Africa, and Europe had learned to farm. They had tamed the wild cattle, horses, sheep, and pigs; and they grew wheat and oats, vegetables and fruit. Then they did not need to fish and hunt and follow the animals around. So they built good houses and lived on their farms and in towns. They had schools, too. They could read and write and do arithmetic just as you can.

These long ago people knew many things that you know, but they did not know that the earth is a globe. The earth looks flat, so they thought it was flat like a table. When the scientists said that the earth is a globe, the other people laughed at them.

"Why," they said, "if it were a globe the people on the under side would be standing on their heads. They would fall off!"

"That is silly," they said, and laughed.

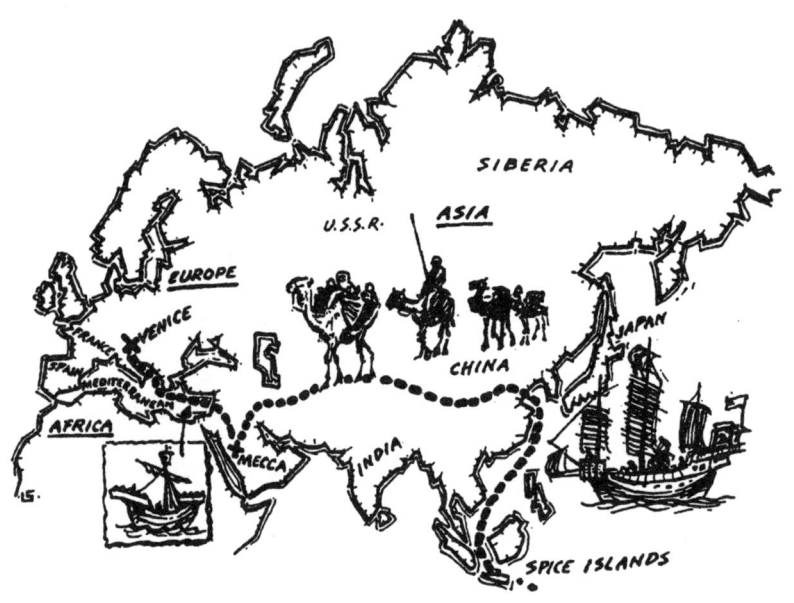

The people of Europe grew most of their food, but they did not grow spices, like pepper and cinnamon. They did not grow sugar, either. They had only a little honey to sweeten their food, and no candy. Think of that, no candy!

The Europeans got their sugar, pepper, and other spices from the East India Islands in Asia. They called them the "Spice Islands". The Asians carried the sugar and spices on camels to Mecca. The European sailors brought them in ships from the coast near Mecca to Venice. The merchants in Venice got rich selling them to the Europeans.

Then there was a war. The sailors could not go to trade with the people of Mecca. The merchants had no sugar and spices to sell.

"Go round the other way," said the scientists. "If the world is a globe you can sail round it. You can sail west across the Atlantic Ocean to Asia and the Spice Islands, and get your sugar and spices."

The scientists did not know that there was a continent of America and a Pacific Ocean on the earth. They thought that if the earth were a globe, Asia and the Spice Islands must be just on the other side of the Atlantic Ocean. And so they would have been if there had been no America and Pacific Ocean in between.

**2. Christopher Columbus discovered America in 1492.**

Christopher Columbus was an Italian boy who became a sailor when he was fourteen years old. He liked geography, and studied hard at it until he was pretty sure that the earth is a globe. He, too, thought that Asia and the Spice Islands must be just on the other side of the Atlantic Ocean. He wanted very much to sail across and find out, but he had no money to buy a ship and hire sailors. He asked several Kings for a ship, but none of them would give him one. At last he asked Queen Isabella of Spain and she gave him the money to buy three ships, the *Pinta*, the *Nina*, and the *Santa Maria*.

When the ships were ready, Columbus steered boldly out into the Atlantic Ocean. Probably the sailors thought about the edge of the earth table and the monsters under it and prayed hard, but Columbus kept the ships headed straight west.

QUEEN ISABELLA OF SPAIN

The sea was smooth, the sun shone, a gentle wind blew them steadily west. At first the sailors liked the wind, but as the weeks went by and it kept blowing them west, they were frightened. The ships of those days had no engines, only sails, and the men were afraid that if this wind blew always west they would never get home again.

"And by this time", they whispered to each other, "we must be very near the edge." Think how frightened they must have been! They begged Columbus to turn back, but he persuaded them to go on a little longer and they did. They were brave men.

Suddenly, one day after they had sailed for about six weeks, a sailor on the *Nina* gave a great shout. Everyone came running and he showed them a green branch with fresh berries on it floating in the sea. They knew then that they were near land, and all was joy and excitement. At two o'clock in the morning, Tirana, the watchman, saw the moonlight shining brightly on a white shore.

Early the next morning, Columbus put on his scarlet cloak and gold chain. He took his sword in one hand and the Spanish flag in the other, and his men rowed him to the shore. They found themselves on an island, beautiful with flowers and trees, and with brown-skinned people peeping from among them.

Columbus and his men knelt and thanked God for bringing them safe to the new land. Then Columbus took possession of it for Queen Isabella of Spain. He thought he had reached the East India Islands in Asia, so he called the people Indians.

When Columbus got home, he was received with great joy and pride. The King and Queen sent for him. He rode to meet them dressed in scarlet, riding on a white horse. He told the King that he had reached the Spice Islands and showed him the gold, strange fruits, and the

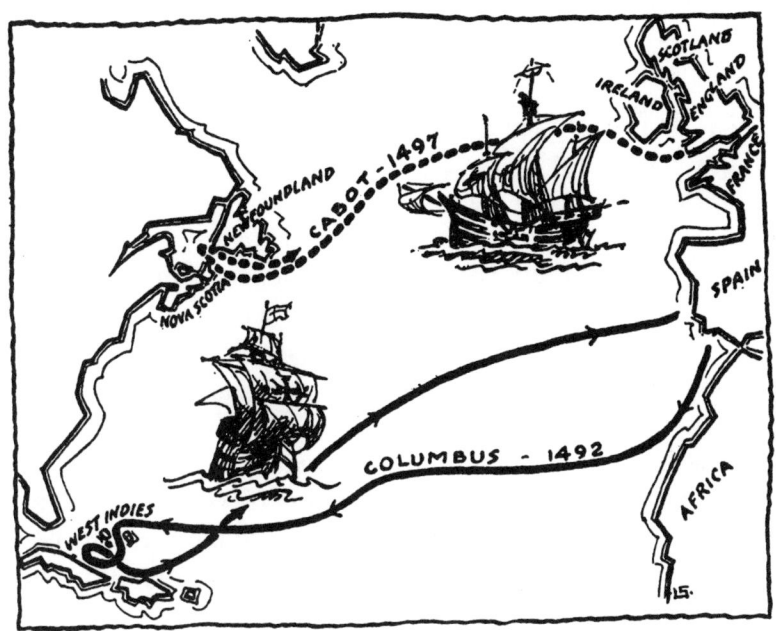

Indians whom he had brought home with him. The King gave him rich gifts and made him an admiral.

Columbus made three more voyages to America before he died, but he never did find out that he had not reached the East Indies. Instead, he had found the West Indies and discovered the great new continent of America.

**3. John Cabot discovered Canada in 1497.**

John Cabot was another Italian sailor who believed that the earth was a globe. He had sailed to trade in Mecca for silks and spices. He had talked to the camel drivers and they had told him what a long, long way it was across Asia to the Spice Islands. Cabot thought it would be shorter to cross the Atlantic to reach them.

Like the scientists, Cabot did not know that there was a continent of America and a Pacific Ocean.

At first he tried to convince the King of France to give him money for a voyage west. But at that time the King of France was not interested.

"If I were in England," Cabot thought, "I could sail across to Asia quite easily." So he went to Bristol on the west shore of England.

The Bristol men were great sailors. When Cabot explained his plan to them they were eager to go with him. The Bristol merchants gave Cabot a small ship. He took his sons and eighteen men and away they sailed to the west. Cabot knew from Columbus' voyage that the Spice Islands were there, somewhere in the west, so he and his men were not afraid that they would sail over the edge of the earth.

At last, one day as they were sailing along with a good breeze behind them, the ship began to slow down and they found that they were sailing through a school of large fish. The sailors ran for a basket, put a stone in it, tied a rope to the handle, and let it down. They drew it up full of fish. As they had not had any fresh meat for a long time, the fish were a great treat.

CABOT DISCOVERED NORTH AMERICA

Cabot and his men sailed on and one morning soon after, the steersman shouted "Land!" They all rushed on deck and there, quite near, lay a high, rocky shore. They cheered and clapped each other on the back. Then they stood for a long time looking at the new land.

They did not know it, but they were looking at Canada, our country. Like Columbus, Cabot and his men thought that they had reached the East Indies, in Asia. They looked round but found no sugar, spices, silks, or jewels. They saw no people, but they found snares set for rabbits, and one of the men was nearly caught in a deer trap. So they knew that there must be people living there. Cabot claimed the land for England and, to show that it was hers, he set up a big wooden cross with the King of England's crest on it.

When they returned to England, Cabot told King Henry and the merchants that they had reached the East Indies, and asked for more ships to go back the next year to trade. The Bristol merchants then gave him the ships and he went back. But still he found no people to trade with and no sign of gold or spices, so he and his men never came back to our country again.

# 3  How White Men Came to Live in Canada
### 1500 to 1600

**1. French fishermen found the way in.**

By this time, many fishermen were sailing across the Atlantic Ocean to fish where the fish were so thick in the sea near Cabot's New Found Land. The men slept on their little sailing ships, and every morning they took their rowboats out to fish. When they had their boats full they rowed back and threw the fish up onto the deck of their ship. They cleaned the fish and dropped them into barrels of salt water to keep them from spoiling. When they had finished they had their supper and went to bed.

At first they were afraid to go ashore. They could hear wild cries and roarings coming from the land, and they thought that there must be devils living there. Then one day big waves drove one of the rowboats ashore, and the fishermen found that the roarings were made by the waves rushing into caves in the rocks.

After that they knew there were no devils on the land, so they began to go ashore to dry their fish in the hot summer sun. The dried fish tasted better than the salted ones; and dried fish are lighter and will last longer. Drying fish was more work; but the fishermen could now return home with more and better fish.

Soon there were fishermen drying their fish all along that shore. It had not been named then. The fishermen just called it "The New Found Land". We call it Newfoundland.

Each spring the boats raced for the beaches that had the most sun for drying the fish. The men built huts for themselves and long tables, called stages, and spread the fish out on them to dry. They turned first one side of the fish up to the sun and then the other. When the fish were dry they stacked them up in little piles. When a captain had his ship full of dried fish, he sailed her home for the winter.

At first the captains took all their men home in the fall. But the winter storms blew down their huts and stages, so the captains began to leave two or three men at each drying ground to take care of their buildings. Some of these men liked our country and stayed here. They were our first settlers.

The French fishermen fished round the north end of the New Found Land. One summer one bold lad sailed right round the north end of it, on through a narrow strait and out into a wide gulf. The water was quieter there and the fish were smaller, but they had finer flesh. The sun was hot for drying, and the woods along the shore gave the men timber to build huts and stages.

THE FISHERMEN DRYING THEIR FISH

After that more and more French fishermen fished in the Gulf behind Newfoundland. Two or three of them even sailed up a large river which they found flowing into it. The Indians up the river called it the River of Canada. They called their country Canada. Canada is now our country, too. The French fishermen had got inside it and had found out its name.

**2. Jacques Cartier's men traded buttons for furs and drank down a spruce tree in 1534.**

By this time the sailors had found that central America is very narrow, so they supposed that all America was narrow. They were still looking for a short waterway through it to the Spice Islands. When the French King heard of the River of Canada which his fishermen had found, he thought it might be the short cut. He sent Jacques Cartier to find out if it was.

Cartier lived in St. Malo, one of the French fishing towns. The fishermen told him how to get round Newfoundland into the Gulf and River of Canada. The King gave him two ships and sixty-one men, and they sailed away to see what they could find.

They got into the Gulf and sailed across it into a large bay where they went ashore. It was hot, but the woods were shady. They found green fields with ripe strawberries, and a river with salmon in it. They called their bay Bay Chaleur (Hot Bay). The next day some Indians came down to the shore, held up furs, and waved to the white men to come and trade. The sailors rowed over and traded a knife, or hatchet, or even a brass button for a fine beaver skin worth a great deal more. The Frenchmen traded all the buttons off their coats. The

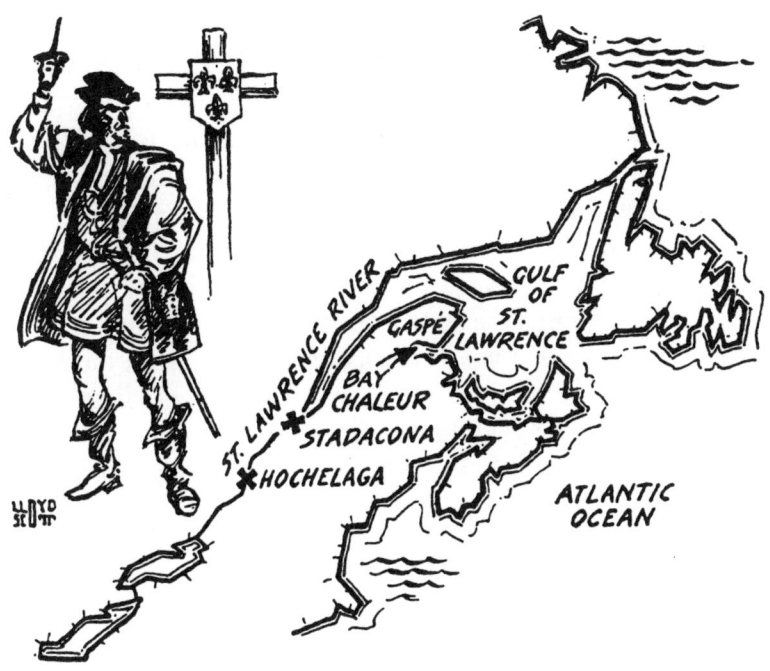

Indians traded all the furs they had on and ran away naked.

Cartier set up a tall cross with the King's crest on it to show that they were Christians and that he had taken the land for the King of France. When he had done this, all the Frenchmen knelt down and thanked God for this beautiful land of Canada which they had found.

Cartier went home to France for the winter, but he came back to Canada the next year. This time he sailed up the River of Canada. He named it the St. Lawrence, and sailed up to the Indian villages of Stadacona and Hochelaga. In both places the Indians welcomed the visitors. At Hochelaga, the Indians told Cartier that he could not take his ships farther up the river. They said that above their little village the river was full of rapids, and that devils lived there. So Cartier turned back.

When he reached Stadacona again, the St. Lawrence was frozen. The Frenchmen had to stay there all winter. It was very cold and their clothes were not warm enough. Many of them became sick with scurvy, a disease which comes from eating salt meat with no green vegetables or fruit. Twenty-five of them died. Then Cartier met an old Indian who told him to give his sick men tea made of spruce bark. Sure enough the spruce tea cured them. That winter they drank down a whole spruce tree. As soon as the ice cleared out on the river, the Frenchmen sailed for sunny France, and very glad they were to get there.

Then there was a war. All the Frenchmen had to stay at home and fight. None of them came back to Canada for a long time.

**3. Sir Humphrey Gilbert took Newfoundland for England in 1583.**

While the French were fighting at home, the English took Newfoundland. Because John Cabot had discovered it, the English said that all North America belonged to England. France and Spain said they had a right to part of it and, as you see on the map, they each took a part.

By this time over three hundred fishing boats from the different countries were sailing over every spring to fish round Cabot's New Found Land. St. John's

18

harbour was their centre. Every week the fishermen chose one of their captains to rule the harbour for that week. They called him their "Admiral".

When Queen Elizabeth I of England heard how many boats were fishing round Newfoundland, she was afraid that France or Spain would take it too. So she sent Sir Humphrey Gilbert to take it for England. Sir Humphrey sold part of his land to get money to buy five ships and hire two hundred and fifty men. One of his ships sailed off to be a pirate, but the other four reached St. John's harbour on a fine, bright August morning. When Gilbert asked for fresh food the fishermen gave him a great feast of salmon, lobster, and fresh raspberries; with biscuits, marmalade, and wine given by the Portuguese fishermen.

The next day Gilbert set up a tent on a little hill. He called the captains of all the ships round him and read the Queen's letter in a loud voice. One of his men dug up a piece of sod and gave it to Gilbert to take to the Queen to show her that Newfoundland now belonged to England. Gilbert and the English sailors had a meeting and made some rules. One said that if anyone spoke rudely of Queen Elizabeth his ears would be cut off. The sailors set up a post with the Queen's crest on it and the party was over.

In September Gilbert sailed south to take possession of other parts of America for England. The weather was very stormy and many of the men were sick. Sir Humphrey put all the sick ones on the big *Swallow* and sent her home to England. He himself went on board the little *Squirrel*.

The storm drove the ships among rocks and sand banks. The big *Delight* stuck fast, but the *Golden Hind* and the little *Squirrel* got away. The *Delight* sank, but her men rowed ashore in their small boats and at last got home to England. The *Golden Hind* and the *Squirrel* ran into a great storm. The men were terribly frightened, but they could see Sir Humphrey sitting quietly on the deck of the little *Squirrel* and hear him calling to them, "We are as near to Heaven by sea as by land."

Then a huge wave fell upon the little *Squirrel* and buried her under the sea. Of all Sir Humphrey's five fine ships only the *Golden Hind* reached England to tell that brave story.

### 4. Sir Francis Drake took the west coast for England in 1579.

Because Columbus had discovered America, Spain claimed all North and South America. Her soldiers killed many southern Indians and carried home shiploads of their gold, silver, and jewels. The English thought that they should have a share of these treasures, so bold English captains sailed out to fight the Spanish ships. They captured many of them and took the gold and pearls for England.

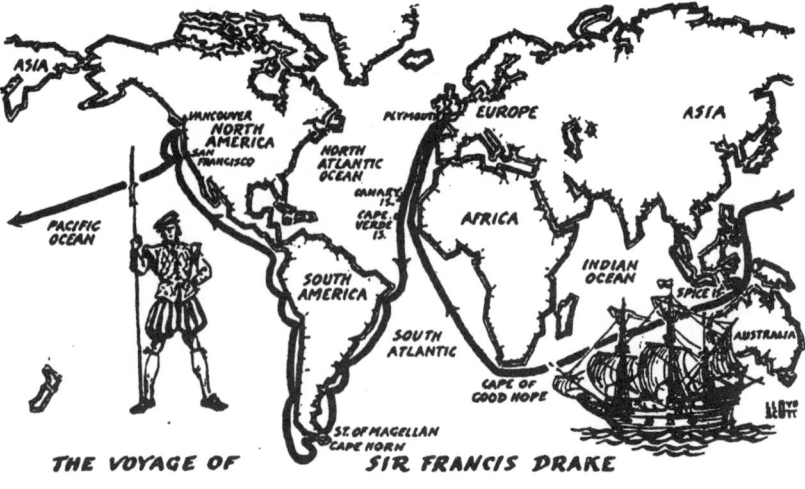

THE VOYAGE OF SIR FRANCIS DRAKE

The boldest of these English treasure hunters was young Francis Drake. He had taken so many of their ships that the Spanish called him the "master thief". But the English were very proud of him.

Then Drake thought, "Why not take part of the treasure country for England! Then we could bring home our own gold and jewels." So he got ready five small ships, and men to sail them. To keep his plan secret from the Spanish, he sailed south to Africa. Then he turned west and headed for South America.

After many adventures Drake and his men came to the Strait of Magellan where the weather is very bad. Drake's ship got through it, but the other four ships did not. From there on he had only his own *Golden Hind* to depend on. But he and his men sailed boldly up the west coast of South America. They did not kill anyone, but they often landed and seized whatever treasure they could find: gold, silver, jewels, rich clothes, food, and wine.

They were chased by two large Spanish ships. Drake could not fight them so the *Golden Hind* fled. For a day and a night they raced north with the big ships after them. The wind was high and the ships rolled among the great waves. The Spanish sailors were sick. They gave up and turned back.

By this time the *Golden Hind*'s hold was stuffed full of treasure. Drake was ready to go home, but he dared not go back through the Strait of Magellan, for dozens of Spanish ships were waiting for him in the Atlantic. There must surely be some northern waterway through America. Drake sailed north till the weather became so cold that his sails were coated with ice and his men were freezing, but they did not find a way through.

There was just one thing to do: they must sail across the Pacific and round the world home. So they sailed

DRAKE AND HIS MEN REPAIR THE *Golden Hind*

south till they found a pleasant little bay where the men could repair the *Golden Hind*. While they worked on her, Drake made friends with the Indians. They had never seen white men before. They thought that the Englishmen were gods and brought them gifts.

Before they left, Drake took possession of all that coast for England. He had one of his men cut Queen Elizabeth's name and the date into a small lead plate, and nail it to a strong post. This was to show that this land now belonged to England. Then he and his men sailed across the Pacific and Indian Oceans, round South Africa, and got safely home. Queen Elizabeth went to Plymouth to meet them, and there before a great company, she made Drake kneel. Then she touched his shoulder with her golden sword and said, "Rise, Sir Francis Drake." She had made him a knight.

No one knows just how far north along the west coast of America Drake sailed. But if his sails froze it may have been at least as far as our British Columbia. So Newfoundland and British Columbia, our farthest east and farthest west provinces, were the first parts of Canada to be claimed by the British.

# 4
## At First Canada Was All French
### 1600 to 1612

**1. Champlain reported on Canada.**

At last the war in France was over and the French soldiers returned to their homes. One of them was Samuel Champlain. He got a job on a ship sailing to America. When he came home he wrote a book about his travels to the New World. When the King heard about this he invited Champlain to his court. There the young seaman told the King about his trip. He said that America was a fine country and that France should have a share of it.

The King said he certainly must have a share of America. He remembered that Cartier had taken Canada for France, and decided to build a settlement there. Trader Pontgrave was going to Canada to trade for furs with the Indians, so the King sent Champlain with him to look over the country and report on it.

Pontgrave and Champlain sailed to Tadoussac, a place where the Indians came to trade with the fishermen. While Pontgrave traded, Champlain took a small boat up the river to the rapids. The Indians there drew him a picture of the river farther on. It showed the river flowing out of a great water. Champlain was tremendously excited. Like Cartier, he thought that perhaps this river was the short way through America to the Pacific Ocean that the sailors were looking for.

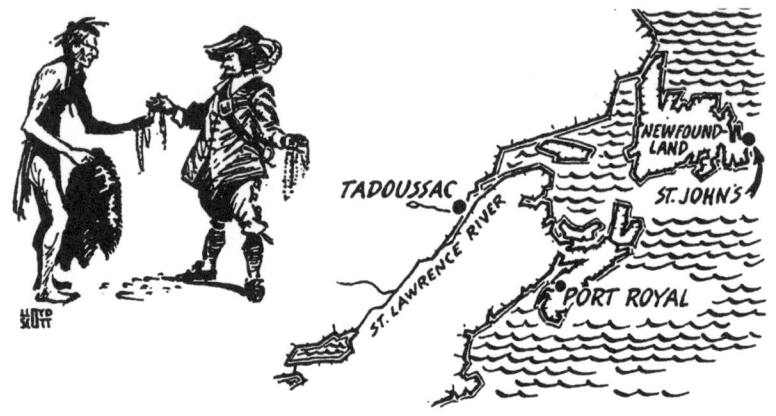

**THE FUR TRADE BEGINS AT TADOUSSAC**

He hurried back to Tadoussac where Pontgrave had collected a shipload of fine furs and they raced the ship home to France. When the King saw the beautiful furs Pontgrave had brought home, and heard Champlain's report of the great size and beauty of Canada and of the great river leading west, he was eager to build a settlement there and to find a way through Canada to the Pacific Ocean.

## 2. De Monts built Port Royal in 1605.

De Monts, a rich man, said he would build the settlement in Canada if the King would give him a monopoly of the fur trade. A monopoly is permission to be the only person allowed to buy or sell a certain thing, like furs, or salt, or candy. The person who has a monopoly can make a great deal of money. The King gave De Monts a monopoly of the fur trade.

De Monts decided to build the settlement in Acadia (the Atlantic coast region) because it is nearer France than the St. Lawrence is. While Pontgrave went to trade at Tadoussac, De Monts and Champlain with sixty settlers sailed round the part we call Nova Scotia, looking for a good place to build a fur trading post. They chose a beautiful bay that Champlain had discovered, and built their houses round a square. They built a storehouse, and surrounded their little fort with a palisade (strong fence). They named it Port Royal; it was the first settlement of white men on the mainland of Canada.

De Monts gave the land round Port Royal to Poutrincourt, a nobleman who wanted to live there. He planted wheat on his land, and the men planted vegetable gardens. The wheat and vegetables grew well. The settlers ate the vegetables with their meat and no one was sick.

But the fishermen-fur traders were angry because the King had given De Monts the monopoly. They could not trade in furs now, as they had been doing for a hundred years. They persuaded the King to take back the monopoly. De Monts could not afford to keep up the settlement without it, so Port Royal had to be given up. Sadly the settlers said good-bye to their fort and their gardens, and sailed home to France.

### 3. Champlain built Quebec and fought the Iroquois.

Champlain did not give up; he was not that kind of man. He was determined that this beautiful Canada should belong to France. He persuaded De Monts to build a settlement far up the St. Lawrence River where the fishermen did not go. The King gave De Monts a monopoly of the fur trade there for one year and away they sailed; Champlain was the captain of one ship, and Pontgrave of the other.

MAKING THE GARDEN AT PORT ROYAL

Pontgrave reached Tadoussac first and what did he find but a pirate ship trading with the Indians for furs. The pirates attacked Pontgrave and had just boarded his ship and seized him when, luckily, Champlain arrived with his ship. That made it two against one, so the pirates sailed off. While Pontgrave traded with the Indians at Tadoussac, Champlain went on up to Stadacona to build a fort. He chose a place where a high cliff juts out into the river. The Indians called it Quebec, which means the "place where the river narrows". There was a strip of land at the foot of the cliff, and Champlain thought his settlement would be safe there with the cliff behind it. They built the fort in 1608 and Champlain planted a garden round it. When the buildings were finished, the men built a strong wooden wall round them and set three cannon on it.

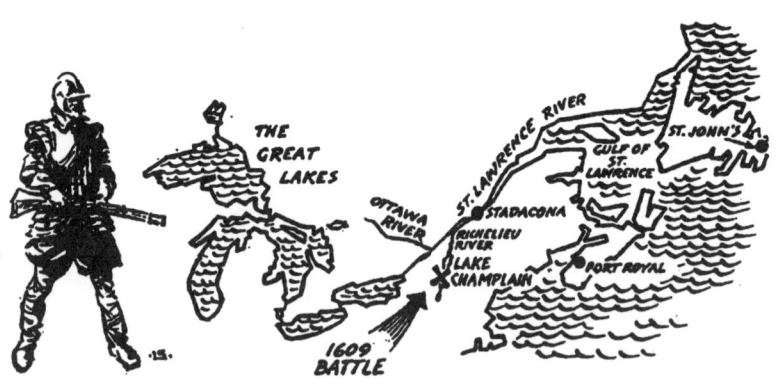

THE ROAD TO THE IROQUOIS COUNTRY

While they were building, three of the workmen made a plot to kill Champlain. They planned to shout "fire" outside Champlain's tent and, when he rushed out, to kill him. But one of the good workmen heard the men plotting this wicked deed and told Champlain. He seized the plotters and sent them to France to be punished.

In September Pontgrave took the furs to France, leaving Champlain and twenty-seven men to hold Quebec. One bright fall day a young Ottawa Indian paddled up to Quebec. Champlain showed him the fort and its guns. The Indian, who had never before seen guns, thought them magic. He begged Champlain to go with his tribe to fight against the fierce Iroquois. Champlain promised to do this if the Indians would guide him in exploring the country farther west. The Indian promised to do this.

So, in the spring, Champlain and his men joined a party of Huron Indians on their way south to fight the Iroquois. They paddled up a fine river which Champlain named Richelieu, and came to a lake now called Lake Champlain.

Near the lake they met the Iroquois and the arrows flew thick and fast. Then Champlain raised his gun and fired. Two Iroquois chiefs fell dead. The Iroquois, who had never seen guns, were terrified and fled. Champlain was sorry that he had made enemies of the Iroquois; he knew that he would not be able to explore their lands.

But the Canadian Indians were delighted. They wanted to take Champlain home with them to show him the "Great Sea", which lay west of their country. Champlain thought that it might be the Pacific Ocean and he was eager to go, but he could not go that year. He had to go to France to report to the King. Instead he sent young Etienne Brule and several other young Frenchmen

27

CHAMPLAIN RAISED HIS GUN

to live with the Indians, and find out as much as they could about their country.

**4. John Guy built Cupids and picnicked with the Beothuks in 1610.**

After Sir Humphrey had taken possession of Newfoundland for Queen Elizabeth I, the fish merchants of Bristol formed a trading company and sent out Governor John Guy to build a settlement in Newfoundland. He brought forty-one settlers and they settled at Cupids. They built houses for themselves, storehouses for their supplies, and a fort to protect their settlement. There were farmers among them and they cleared land for their cattle. In the spring they planted grain.

After he had settled his people and set them to work, Guy sailed along the coast exploring. Beside Trinity Bay the sailors found a copper kettle and some furs. It looked as if the local natives had seen them coming and had hidden. Guy put a few beads and biscuits into the kettle, sailed a little way off, and waited. Sure enough, a party of Indians appeared, waving a wolfskin as a flag. Guy sent a man waving his flag to meet them. Two Indians came

THIS IS THE KIND OF CANNON USED IN CHAMPLAIN'S TIME

forward and presented the English with a knife and a leather chain. Guy gave them a cap, a towel, and a knife. Then they all sat down and picnicked together on dried caribou meat brought by the Indians, and bread, raisins, and wine brought by the English. Guy promised the Indians that the next year he would come back with goods to trade, and both parties left well pleased.

The next year a dreadful thing happened. Another English ship, whose captain did not know of Guy's promise, sailed into Trinity Bay. The Indians rushed down in a crowd to meet her. The captain thought they were going to attack him and fired a cannon at them. The story does not tell whether any of them were killed, but they fled in terror. Probably the Indians thought that it was Guy and that he had betrayed them. They must have believed that he had broken his promise and laid a trap for them. After that, although some Indians were friendly and helped the white men, others did them all the harm they could by stealing and destroying their goods.

## 5. Henry Hudson discovered Hudson Bay in 1610.

While Champlain was in France, he heard exciting news. People said that Henry Hudson, sailing for England, had found a way round the north end of America to the Pacific. Brave English sailors had been searching for this way for years, but they had all been stopped by the ice. At last two English merchants asked Henry Hudson to try to find a passage through to the Pacific, China, and the Spice Islands.

They chose Hudson because he had already made some voyages of exploration to North America. On one of his trips he had discovered the Hudson River. Hudson agreed and took his ten-year-old son, John, with him.

The voyage went well until they got among the great ice floes west of Greenland. After that it was hard going. Often they had to anchor the ship to an ice floe ahead of them and move her forward by pulling on the anchor ropes. At last they came to a strait between two hills. The men went ashore to shoot birds, but returned quickly to tell Hudson that they could see clear water ahead. They sailed forward and came out into a great sea which they thought was part of the Pacific Ocean. We call it Hudson Bay.

They sailed south till they came to the end of the water. By this time the ice was forming, so they had to spend the winter there. They managed fairly well until spring, but by the time they started home they had very little food left. The sailors blamed Hudson for this and they put him, his little son, and a few sailors who were loyal to their captain, into a small boat and left them. They were never seen again.

THE CRUEL SAILORS FORCED HUDSON'S SON INTO THE BOAT

Most of these cruel mutineers died on the way home. Only a few were left to tell of the great discovery Hudson had made. For a while everyone thought that Hudson Bay was part of the Pacific Ocean and that Hudson had found a short way to it round America.

# 5 The Settlers Worked Hard to Get a Start
## 1610-1642

**1. Champlain laid out the fur trade trail to the west.**

Champlain was in France when he heard that Henry Hudson had discovered Hudson Bay. The news made Champlain sad, for he had hoped to be the one to find the short way through America to the Pacific. Then Nicholas Vignau, one of the young men he had sent to live with the Hurons, arrived from Canada. He told Champlain that he had gone with the Hurons to their "Great Sea" and that it was the Pacific.

When he heard this, Champlain hurried back to Canada and paddled up the Ottawa River till he came to the camp of Chief Tessouat. Champlain asked the Chief to lend him canoes to carry him and his men on to the country of the Nipissings.

"You must not go to them," said the Chief, "they are a fierce tribe and will kill you."

"Nicholas was among them," said Champlain, "and they did not kill him."

"Nicholas!" roared the Chief. "Did you tell the White Chief that you had been among the Nipissings?"

"Yes, I was there," said Nicholas boldly.

"You are a wicked liar," said the Chief. "You never left my camp. Your master ought to kill you for lying to him as you have done."

Vignau then admitted that he had never gone to the Nipissings' country. Champlain dismissed him in disgrace.

Champlain still hoped that the "Great Sea" the Hurons talked about might be the Pacific. So the next spring he went up the Ottawa, across to Lake Nipissing, and down the French River to the "Great Sea of the Hurons". It looked large enough to be a sea, but when Champlain tasted the water it was fresh. It was only a lake after all.

That was another great disappointment, but Champlain did not give up his plan to build up the fur trade. He met Etienne Brule, heard his report about the lands to the west, and arranged with the chiefs to bring their furs to Canada.

So that the Hurons would not have to bring their furs all the way down to Quebec, Champlain built a trading post at Three Rivers. After that a Fur Fair was held there every summer. The Indians brought their furs down the Ottawa in a great fleet of canoes. At Three Rivers the Company's traders waited, ready to show their goods. There were speeches, gifts, and a great feast. Next day the trading began. It went on for a week. The Fur Fair was a great help to both the Indians and the fur traders.

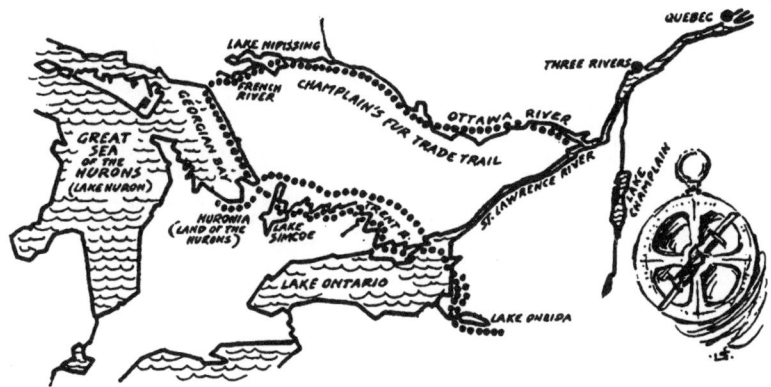

CHAMPLAIN'S FUR TRADE TRAIL

## 2. The English took Acadia, but the French took her back.

By this time Poutrincourt had returned to Port Royal with his son, Biencourt. Claude de la Tour with his son, Charles, settled nearby and a few other settlers also arrived. They had just built houses when an English ship under Captain Argall came sailing up. She came from Virginia, where an English Company had built a settlement.

The English still claimed all of North America, so when the Governor of Virginia heard that the French had settled at Port Royal he sent Captain Argall to drive them away. Poutrincourt and his men fought for their lands, but the English won. They took the Frenchmen to Virginia, but later allowed them to go back to France.

The English attack did not drive the French away for ever; they soon went back to Port Royal. Poutrincourt, who had returned to France for good, gave Port Royal to his son Biencourt. Biencourt had decided to become a fur

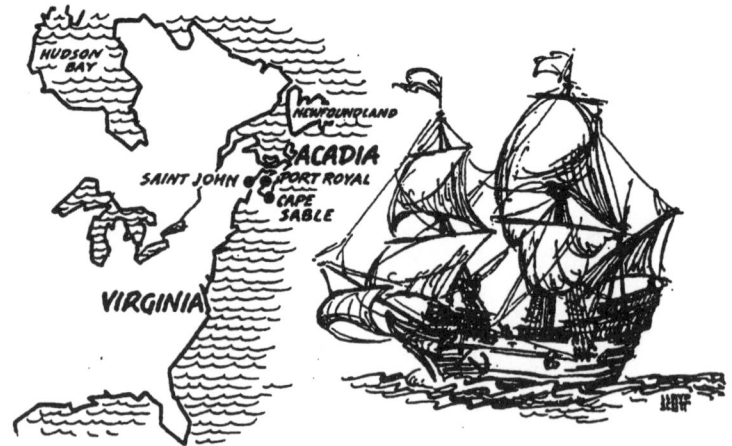

THE ENGLISH CALLED THEIR SECOND COLONY VIRGINIA

trader, and he and Charles la Tour each chose a good place and built his own trading post. Biencourt had two posts, Port Royal and Cape Sable. When he died, he left them to his friend, Charles la Tour, who had his post at Saint John. With three trading posts, Charles la Tour was the leading fur trader in Acadia.

**3. Quebec had the first church and school.**

On one of his trips to France, Champlain brought back four priests to preach to the Canadians and to christianize the Indians. The very day after they landed at Quebec the four Fathers tucked up their long black robes under their rope girdles and began to build Canada's first church. It was a very little church, and the Fathers soon finished it.

Father Jean de Brebeuf was chosen to build a Mission among the Hurons. He went home with the Indians after the Fur Fair in Three Rivers. He was a big man and strong, but the Indians nearly wore him out. They teased him and laughed at him, gave him very little to eat, and kept him paddling all day long.

The Fathers built their Mission House like a Huron long house, longer than it was wide. It was framed of poles planted in the ground with the ends bent into an arch for the roof, lashed together with cross-poles, and covered with sheets of bark. The priests divided their house into three rooms: hall, kitchen-bedroom, and chapel. This astonished the Indians, whose long houses consisted of one room with a row of fires down the middle, one for each family. The Fathers' only furniture was a few stools, a handmill, and a clock. The Indians were delighted with the clock and would sit for hours waiting to hear it strike.

"What does the Captain say?" they would ask.

THE FATHERS BUILD THEIR LONG HOUSE

"When he strikes twelve times he says, 'Hang on the kettle'," answered the Father. "When he strikes four times he says, 'Get up and go home'." The Indians always obeyed the Captain, so after four o'clock the Fathers had a little time to rest.

**4. Father Jogues was a hero.**

Father Jogues and his Huron friends were paddling back with supplies for the Mission when the Mohawks, one of the six Iroquois tribes, caught them. Jogues swam to shore and might have escaped, but when he saw that his Indians had been captured, he gave himself up.

The Iroquois took their prisoners to their village in the Mohawk country. The women and children rushed out to meet them. They formed two long lines and forced the prisoners to run between them. As they ran the women whipped them so hard that Jogues fainted. They dragged him in and placed him with the others on a platform where the Indians cut at them with their knives.

Father Jogues lived with the Mohawks for a year. Then they took him with them to trade at Fort Orange, a Dutch town. The Dutch people advised Jogues to escape to a French ship in the river. He was very lame, but while the Iroquois slept he managed to hobble the half mile to the river bank. He pushed a boat into the water, and rowed

RUNNING THE GAUNTLET

over to the ship. The sailors helped him on board and hid him. When the Indians woke and found Jogues gone, they were very angry. They searched the ships but did not find him and he got safely to France.

In 1644, Jogues returned to Canada. The Governor wanted a man to go to make peace with the Iroquois. Jogues could speak Iroquoian so he asked him to go. Jogues was a brave man. He went straight back to the Mohawks who had treated him so cruelly. The Indians now wanted to stop fighting, so they received Jogues kindly and made a treaty of peace. Jogues took it to Quebec and then went back to try to convert the Mohawks.

It was a very dry summer. The Iroquois' corn crop failed and there was much sickness. The Indians blamed this on a small box that Father Jogues had left in his wigwam. They said it was a magic box and that he had left it behind to kill them. When Father Jogues returned they invited him to a feast. As he entered the door, they struck off his head with a tomahawk. So died one of the bravest Canadians.

# 6 Both English and French Colonies Had to Fight for Their Lives
### 1612 to 1660

**1. The Newfoundlanders fought the pirates.**

All this time the Newfoundlanders were fighting the pirates. Pirate ships were thick on the sea in those days, and they swarmed round Newfoundland. When Sir Richard Whitbourne came from England to hold court and judge evil-doers in Newfoundland, pirate Peter Easton seized him and held him prisoner for eleven days. Pirate Sir Henry Mainwaring robbed the fishermen of their food and fish. He seized French ships and sold them with their cargoes. He kidnapped at least a hundred fishermen. Sir Richard did his best for the Newfoundlanders, but he could not stop the pirates.

**2. The Acadians fought each other.**

At about this time the King of France sent a Governor to Acadia. He settled at La Have. He left Charles la Tour in charge of the trading post at Saint John, but gave Port Royal to a new man named Charnisay. Charnisay brought

CHARNISAY MOCKS LADY LA TOUR

out twenty families and helped them to settle on their farms. He was good to his own people, but he quarrelled with Charles la Tour.

Charnisay waited until he knew that La Tour was away on a trading ship and then he attacked Saint John. Lady la Tour had very few men, but she fought him off for three days. Even then Charnisay had to trick her. He got a traitor in the fort to let his men over the wall in the night. Lady la Tour with her few men fought so fiercely that Charnisay begged her to surrender to save their lives. She did so. Then that wicked Charnisay put a rope around her neck and forced her to watch while he hanged her men, seized her furs, and sailed away. The poor woman was so shocked by the hangings that she died. Charnisay was soon punished. His canoe overturned and, though he reached shore, he took sick and died.

3. **Good women built a school and a hospital at Quebec.**

By this time many more priests had come to Canada to teach the Indians about God. They were brave men. Fearlessly they went out to the tribes, two together, or one alone. In their letters to their friends in France, the priests told of their exciting adventures and narrow escapes.

People in France read these letters and sent money to help them in their work. Today we can read their letters to find out about life in early Canada.

Madame de la Peltrie, a rich widow, decided to go to Quebec and open a girls' school. She asked Mother Marie to go with her and they went out together. There was smallpox in Quebec when they got there, and the two women were kept busy nursing the sick. But as soon as the sick people were well, Mother Marie started work on the school. It was a long wooden building with fire-places at each end. In winter the two great fires had hard work to keep the frost off the inside walls.

The next few years were hard ones. The Iroquois attacked Quebec, and the convent school burned down. This was a dreadful blow. But as soon as the ashes were cool, Mother Marie and her nuns began to clear away the rubbish. Madame Peltrie took the school children into her house, while everyone in the town helped with food, materials, and building. In a year a new convent and school was built. It is there still, built of stone now, and very famous. You can see it when you go to Quebec.

MADAME DE LA PELTRIE AND MOTHER MARIE

Another rich lady who had read the priests' letters sent out nursing nuns and built a hospital at Quebec. It was built first outside the town, but the Iroquois attacked it so fiercely that the Governor brought the nurses inside the town. They built their new hospital on the edge of the hill where it, too, stands today.

## 4. Ville Marie, the City of Mary

The biggest addition to Canada at this time was the building of Montreal. In France, Dauversiere and Father Olier dreamed that an angel told them to build a Mission on Montreal Island. They collected as much money as they could, twenty tons of food, and quite a large party of people. Maissonneuve, a brave soldier, agreed to lead them, and away they sailed for Quebec.

By this time it was fall and the river was freezing, so they stayed in Quebec all winter. In the spring of 1642 they went up to Montreal Island. They landed and all knelt while Father Vimont prayed that God would bless their settlement. They called it Ville Marie, the "City of Mary", Jesus' mother.

The next morning men and women together began cutting down trees and building cabins. They all worked like beavers and before winter their houses were up and a strong palisade of logs had been built round them. Gentle Jeanne Mance started a hospital, and kind, jolly Marguerite Bourgeoys opened a school. At Christmas the river rose almost to their palisade, but they all prayed hard and the flood went down. To show their thankfulness, Maisonneuve had a large wooden cross made. They carried it up and planted it on the top of the mountain. Ever since then a cross has stood at the top of Mount Royal; nowadays it is a beautiful cross made of lights.

The Huron Missions

## 5. The Iroquois killed the Hurons.

By this time the Fathers had four large Missions among the Hurons: Ste. Marie, St. Joseph, St. Ignace, and St. Louis. At Ste. Marie they had built a church, a school, and a house for themselves. They had a fine farm where they grew wheat and kept cows, pigs, and chickens. The Indians often visited them, so they built a large sleeping house for them. They had a big kitchen, too, where in hard times they fed hundreds of Indians.

In good years the Hurons were now well off. They made a good profit on the furs they took down to the Fur Fair at Three Rivers. They built quite good houses, and some of them grew a little grain. But the Iroquois hated them. They hated the Canadians, too. They remembered that the rich St. Lawrence valley had once been their hunting grounds. They were determined to kill the Hurons, drive out the Canadians, and take back their valley.

PILOT TRAINING HER PUPS

The Iroquois attacked St. Joseph on a Sunday morning when the Hurons were in church. They stole up and shot them through the windows. Father Daniel was killed as he tried to save his people. The Iroquois set fire to the town, and marched off, driving before them hundreds of prisoners to be tortured and killed. The next year they attacked St. Ignace and St. Louis. They set fire to the towns, killed the people, and tortured the priests. Jean Brebeuf and the missionaries are remembered for their bravery and dedication; they gave their lives for the glory of God.

Some of the Hurons escaped to Quebec and settled there. Others fled north to Lake Superior where we shall find them by and by.

**6. The heroes saved Canada.**

The Iroquois had wiped out all except a few hundred Hurons, and in 1660 got ready to wipe out young Canada. When news of their plan reached Montreal, Maisonneuve called in the farmers nearby and set them to work to strengthen the stone wall, carry in all the food, weapons, and ammunition they could gather, and to keep watch day and night.

One of their best watchers was the dog, Pilot, who barked at the sight or smell of an Indian. Every morning she trotted round the wall, sniffing. It was fun to see her teaching her pups to make the rounds on guard. When they played about instead of searching, she cuffed them, and sent them back to work.

When young Dollard heard of the Iroquois' plan, he begged Maisonneuve to let him lead a small party up the Ottawa to stop the Iroquois. Maisonneuve agreed, and sixteen brave lads volunteered. They knelt in the church and vowed to follow Dollard to the death. Then they paddled up to the Long Sault. There they repaired an old palisade of tree trunks and, by good luck, were joined by forty Hurons and Algonkians all eager to fight the Iroquois.

The next day their scouts rushed in with word that the Iroquois were coming, and down the river dashed a great fleet of Iroquois canoes full of fighters. They leaped ashore and attacked the little fort furiously, but the Canadians were ready and drove them off.

The Iroquois broke up the Canadians' canoes, lighted the birch bark, and tried to set fire to the palisade. A hail of bullets kept them at a distance. The Iroquois then built a fort of their own. The Canadians too worked swiftly, setting up an inner wall and filling the space between the wall and the palisade with earth and stones. Night and day, two or three sharp-shooters manned each loop-hole in the double wall.

THE BATTLE AT THE LONG SAULT

The Iroquois were beaten back three times. Then, crouched behind trees and logs, they picked off the Canadians, killing some, wounding others. The "heroes" had no water in the little fort. They dug a hole, but got only a little. Without water, they could not swallow the crushed corn which was all they had to eat. Hunger, thirst, and lack of sleep weakened those who were left, but they carried on, fighting and praying by turns.

On the fourth day, a second band of Iroquois arrived. They made heavy shields of split logs and, covered by them, hacked at the palisade with their hatchets. To drive them off, Dollard crammed an old gun with powder and, putting a fuse in it, tried to throw it over the wall. Alas! it fell back, exploded, and killed several of the defenders. In the confusion that followed, the Iroquois tore a hole in the palisade. Dollard sprang to defend it and was shot down. A few more shots and the battle was over. The "Iroquois Yell" told of the Indian victory.

But Dollard and his comrades did not die in vain. The Iroquois had seen sixteen Canadians and a few Indians hold a log palisade for many days against hundreds of Iroquois warriors. They decided to think it over before attacking Montreal and Quebec, and paddled off to their homes. Canada was saved for that time.

# 7 Canada Began to Grow
## 1658 to 1672

### 1. Radisson and Groseilliers saved Canada's trade.

The Iroquois made no more big attacks on Canada, but they kept on making small raids, killing anyone they could catch. They swarmed over the Huron country (Ontario) so that the western Indians dared not bring their furs down the Ottawa River to the Fair at Three Rivers.

Pierre Radisson and Chouart Groseilliers were Three Rivers' boys. When Radisson was a lad he was captured and tortured by the Iroquois. His fingers were gnawed, the soles of his feet burned, and his thumb was thrust among glowing coals. But he bore it all so bravely and was so full of fun that the Iroquois adopted him. He lived with them for two years. Then he got a chance to escape, and after many exciting adventures reached home.

There he found Groseilliers, now his brother-in-law, out of work. Chouart was a fur trader who had worked for the Fathers at the Huron Missions, and knew the country beyond Lake Huron. But the Iroquois had by this time cut Canada off from the west, and Three Rivers had not a single beaver skin in her storehouses. Canada had no furs, her men no work and so no money to buy supplies.

THE PRAIRIES

"Well," said the two young fellows, "if the Indians are afraid to bring their furs down to us to trade for the goods they need, let us take our goods up to them. We can trade in their country and bring the furs back ourselves!"

They knew that the Governor would forbid them to go, so one dark night they paddled quietly away and joined a party of friendly Indians on their way home to Green Bay on Lake Michigan. They had two fights with the Iroquois but reached Green Bay safely. The two lads spent the winter in the Indian camp there.

The next summer they roamed far and wide over the vast prairies south and west. They were the first white men to see them and, said Radisson, "In all my life I have never seen a finer country. The Indians reap twice in the year. Pumpkins and corn grow well in their gardens. Their arrows are of fish bone, their dishes of wood, and they have a great store of tobacco."

The winter was cold, the coats of the beaver were thick. Radisson and Groseilliers traded cleverly. In the spring they set out for Canada with a rich cargo of furs guarded by five hundred Indian warriors. At the Long Sault they met a large party of Iroquois, but they drove them off and found the little fort where Dollard and his heroes had died only eight days before. If only they had come in time! Sadly they paddled on to Three Rivers and then to Quebec where flags flew, church bells rang, and cannon boomed to welcome them.

When the Governor saw how many furs they had brought, he didn't punish them for leaving without his permission. He made a speech and the people praised and feasted them. Canada could send furs to France again; Canadians had money again to buy the things they needed.

## 2. Radisson and Groseilliers led the English to Hudson Bay.

The brothers had done so well on their first trip west that early the next spring they prepared to make another. But when they asked the Governor for a licence to trade, he refused to give them one unless they promised to give him half the furs they brought back. They were furious. Trading without a licence was punished by a heavy fine, or even death, but they risked it and fled.

WHERE RADISSON AND GROSEILLIERS WENT

They traded that summer with the Indians on the west shore of Lake Superior, spent the winter in the Indian camp, and went down with the tribe in the spring to their summer hunting grounds on Hudson Bay. The brothers returned to Quebec with $300,000 worth of furs. Instead of welcoming them, the greedy Governor fined them for trading without a licence, seized most of their furs, and threw Groseilliers into prison.

The brothers had found the furs so plentiful on Hudson Bay that they had planned to go round by sea to get a shipload of them. So, as soon as Groseilliers got out of jail, they fled to Boston where the New Englanders advised them to go to England and ask King Charles to help them.

King Charles looked at their beautiful furs and was delighted with the story of their exciting adventures. He called in his cousin, Prince Rupert, and several rich London merchants, who all listened eagerly. The King gave the brothers one ship, the merchants gave another. By spring all was ready and they set sail.

Radisson was driven back, but Groseilliers' ship got through to Hudson Bay and sailed south to a river which they named Rupert after the Prince. There they built Fort Charles. Groseilliers snowshoed to the camps to invite the Indians to trade. They came, and in the summer

FORT CHARLES

49

Groseilliers took back to England a shipload of such rich and glossy furs that the merchants at once held a secret meeting to form a company to trade in Hudson Bay. They called themselves the "Adventurers". King Charles gave them a charter, that is a permit to trade. And from that long ago year of 1670 until late in this century, the Adventurers traded and did business in Canada's north. We call them the Hudson's Bay Company. It is the oldest trading company in the world. There are still many Bay stores all across Canada; but in 1990 the company sold its northern trading posts.

The Hudson's Bay Company played a big part in Canada's history; many of its employees were important characters. You will read some good stories about the Company and her men as we go on.

### 3. Talon set Canada on her feet.

By 1663 Canada was growing so fast that the French King sent Intendant Talon to manage her business. Talon was proud of our beautiful country and he worked hard to put her on her feet. He saw that she had plenty of good land, timber, fish, and furs. What she needed, he told the King, was more people. So, in France, the King had his chief Minister collect and send off shiploads of settlers and livestock - cattle, chickens, sheep. Meanwhile, in Canada, Talon laid out farms, and built log houses for these new Canadians.

When he arrived, each new farmer was given a farm with a house, and some tools, food, and clothes to last him till he harvested a crop. Also the King paid him for clearing the first two acres of his land. To pay for all this each farmer had to clear two more acres and build a house for one of the settlers in the next ship. This plan worked

THE ARRIVAL OF THE GIRLS

so well that in two years two thousand people came to Canada.

Most of these first farmers were bachelors. But farmers need wives, so the Governor sent to France for healthy girls, strong enough to do the work on a pioneer farm. Many offered to come, and a shipload was chosen. The girls sailed for Canada in charge of two nuns. They were seasick, but they were young and soon well again, and talking excitedly of their homes and husbands waiting in Canada.

The waiting bachelors were also excited. Many were on the wharf when the ship docked, but the nuns took the girls at once to the convent for a day's rest.

When the bachelors came to the convent, the Mother Superior asked each one how much land he had cleared, what kind of house he had and whether he went to church and did not drink. When the girl came in, each man chose one, talked to her, and told her about his farm and house. If she liked him, she married him. The King gave each bride a wedding present of money and provisions. Ship after ship brought girls to Canada to make homes for her men. And most of them made happy homes, as we shall see.

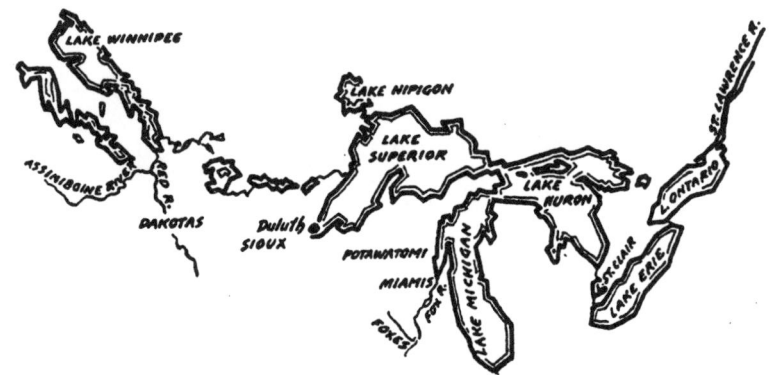

WHERE THE COUREURS DE BOIS TRADED

### 4. The good coureurs worked for Canada.

The coureurs de bois, the "runners of the woods", were young men who ran off to live with the Indians. Many of them were lazy fellows, but some were good men who managed their fur-trading business well. While they traded, they explored the new country, became leaders of the Indians, and kept them loyal to Canada.

Daniel DuLuth was one of the best coureurs de bois. He lived and worked among the Indians south of Lake Superior. He explored that country, and influenced the Indians as far west as the Assiniboine River. Soon after he came to the west, DuLuth found two tribes at war near the city now named after him, Duluth. They had been fighting for years, but DuLuth persuaded them to make peace and to send their furs to Canada. He even persuaded the tribes who had been trading with the Hudson's Bay Company to trade with Canada.

Nicholas Perrot was another good coureur de bois. He was only sixteen years old when he went up to the Indian country with the missionaries. He became a fur trader trading with the Fox, Dakota, Sioux, and Miami tribes. He travelled among them for years and knew more about the south-west Lake Huron country than anyone else. He was an honest trader and a friendly person. His Indians loved and trusted him. He persuaded the western tribes to help Canada against the Iroquois.

**5. The Newfoundlanders fought the fishing admirals.**

All this time the Newfoundlanders had been having very hard times. The rich English fish merchants who sent out their ships to fish along the shores of Newfoundland did not want settlers on the island. They got the English government to make cruel laws against them. Yet in spite of these laws people did settle around the bays and inlets. They fished and farmed and were happy there. In winter they had peace, but in summer the English fishermen came over, seized the Newfoundlanders' fish, destroyed their drying stages, burnt their houses, and even killed people. At last an order came that all settlers should move their homes six miles back from the shore. This was too much for the settlers. They refused to do it, but many did move to new secret harbours where they built houses without chimneys so smoke would not give them away.

Worst of all was the new rule about admirals. The old rule was that in each harbour the captains of the ships there for the summer should, each in turn, be its admiral and rule that harbour for a week. This was not so bad, for if the people had a cruel admiral one week, they might get a good one the next week. The new rule made one captain the ruler for the whole summer. This was good if they had a good admiral, but many of the captains were cruel, greedy men who were very hard on the Newfoundlanders.

## 6. Newcomers in Newfoundland

While England thought only about the rich fishing grounds around Newfoundland and discouraged settlement on the island, France began to think that a colony on the southern shore would be a good thing. It would be a guardian to the colonies on the St. Lawrence and in Acadia, protecting them from the English. So in 1662 French settlers were sent to Placentia Bay.

For about fifty years the two countries fought for control of the island and the surrounding sea - as well as fighting each other in Europe. During this time life became harder and harder for all the settlers. Because of the battles on the sea, few trading ships could get through to bring needed supplies or pick up fish.

Then in 1713 the two countries signed a treaty. The French settlers agreed to leave the island, but French fishermen were allowed to use the southern shore to dry their catch of fish. It became known as the "French Shore".

# 8 Canada Spread North, West, and South
### 1670 to 1690

**1. Talon took possession of the north and west.**

Talon did not stop with building up Canada by bringing in new settlers. He planned to take the whole north, west, and south of North America for Canada and France. When he saw how fast the English settlements in the east were growing, he thought he had better do it right away.

Talon chose Saint-Lusson to take possession of the north-west. Coureur Nicholas Perrot went ahead and had a great crowd of Indians waiting at Sault Ste. Marie when Saint-Lusson arrived. The good Fathers at the Mission set up a big wooden cross, and a post with the King's crest on it, and said a prayer. The French Canadians sang their national song. Then Saint-Lusson stepped forward with his sword in one hand and a sod in the other. In a loud voice he said, "In the name of The Most High, Mighty, Christian King Louis XIV of France, I take possession of this place and all countries, rivers, lakes of the North, West, and South. Vive le Roi!" Then all the Canadians fired their guns and shouted "Vive le Roi!"

The natives who had gathered yelled too, loud and long, although many of them surely didn't understand what was going on. Then the party was over.

**2. Jolliet explored the Mississippi River in 1673.**

Jolliet was the son of a wagon maker in Quebec and he was so friendly and good natured that everybody liked him. He was clever at school, too, and the Fathers wanted him to be a priest. But he loved the woods and became a fur trader and explorer.

Talon chose Jolliet to lead a party to explore the Mississippi, and Father Marquette of the Sault to go with him. They went in two bark canoes with five men, taking with them some smoked meat and corn. Paddling south on Lake Michigan, they met the Wild Rice Indians who told them that the Mississippi was guarded by monsters who would swallow them, canoes and all; but they just laughed at that story and pushed on to Green Bay. From there they portaged across to the Wisconsin River, floated down to its mouth, and steered out into the broad Mississippi.

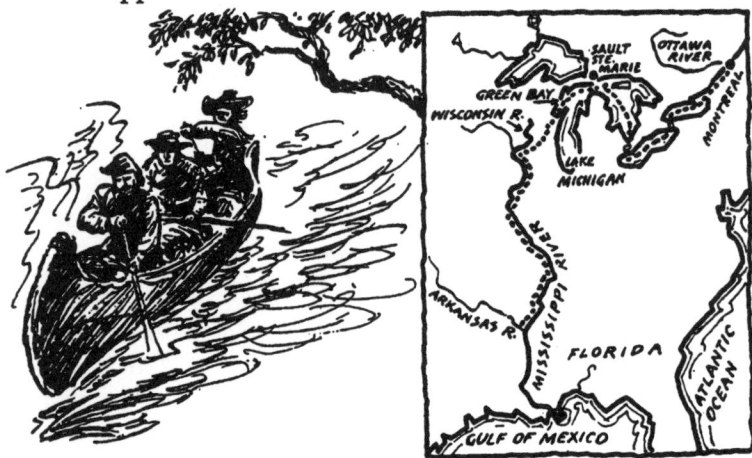

WHERE JOLLIET WENT

They paddled south for two weeks without seeing a single person. Then, one evening when they landed for the night, they saw footprints and followed these till they heard Indians talking. They were afraid, but when they stepped out the Indians just stared at them. Then four chiefs came forward with two peace pipes. After smoking them, the white men were taken to the head chief who stood in his doorway, shading his eyes with his hands.

"Frenchmen," he said, "how bright the sun shines when you come to visit us." The Indians then feasted their guests, gave them peace pipes (calumets), and in the morning took the French Canadians to their canoes.

Day after day the explorers paddled on. It was very hot and the mosquitoes tortured them. The Indians they met now had guns. Some tribes threatened them. The Arkansas Indians feasted them for a whole day to fatten them; they planned to kill and eat them. The chief saved them, but he warned them that the next tribe would be sure to kill them.

Jolliet and Marquette now knew that the Mississippi flows into the Gulf of Mexico. This was what they had really come to find out, so they decided to return. It took

JOLLIET AND THE WILD RICE INDIANS

ten weeks' hard paddling the 2500 miles upstream to reach Green Bay. Marquette was sick and remained there to rest, but Jolliet hurried on to report to the Governor. He had paddled over 5000 miles without an accident, but his canoe capsized in the rapids at Lachine. He escaped with his life, but lost three men and all his maps and papers. Luckily he was able to make a fairly full spoken report.

**3. Governor Frontenac made the Iroquois behave.**

By this time the French King had called Talon home and sent out Governor Frontenac. He was a brave soldier who had fought in many wars, but was now retired and poor. He came to Canada hoping to make money by the fur trade. Frontenac was a big, bold, hot-tempered man who had a wonderful gift for getting on with the Iroquois.

Soon after he came to Canada Frontenac met La Salle, a young Frenchman who had a seigneury on Montreal Island. La Salle's great ambition was to explore the Mississippi to its mouth and take possession of the south of North America for Canada and France. For this he needed money. He went to Frontenac who gave him

The arrival of Frontenac at Fort Frontenac

permission to build a trading post at Lachine. There he hoped to catch up with the Indians on their way to Montreal, buy all their furs, and sell them at a big profit. La Salle named the post Fort Frontenac. Over time it became the city of Kingston, Ontario.

When La Salle was ready to begin building the fort, Frontenac invited the Iroquois to a meeting there. The chief arrived with his braves and they pitched their tents. Then up the river swept a great fleet of canoes full of French soldiers in their bright red and blue uniforms. Next came two flat boats painted scarlet, carrying cannon. Then, in a great canoe gorgeously painted, came Frontenac, dressed in velvet trimmed with gold, his hat covered with sweeping plumes, and with the great white and gold flag of France floating over him. Another fleet of canoes with soldiers followed him. It was the grandest sight the Iroquois had ever seen.

Frontenac landed and received the chiefs politely. He listened to their speeches and gave them rich gifts of tobacco. Then he spoke to them. He said that he was their father and that if they were good children, he would be good to them, but if they were bad, he would punish them severely. The proud, fierce Iroquois admired him. They named him the "Great Onontio", and promised to be his good children. They *were* good while he was Governor.

**4. La Salle took the south-west for Canada in 1682.**

La Salle did make money at Fort Frontenac, but he thought that he could make it faster if he had a ship to bring furs down from the north-west in shiploads, instead of in canoe loads. No one could take a ship over Niagara Falls, so La Salle built his ship, the *Griffin*, above the Falls. He loaded her with goods, and sailed to Mackinac.

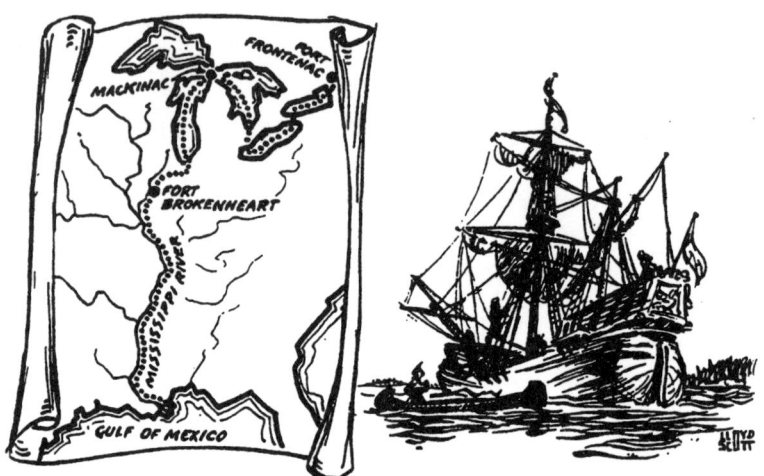

## LA SALLE'S JOURNEY AND THE *Griffin*

There he traded his goods for furs and sent the *Griffin* back with them to Fort Frontenac. His men there were to sell them and send him the money for his explorations. Meantime La Salle and his party went on to build a fort on the Wisconsin River. At this fort, which they afterwards called Fort Brokenheart, they waited for the money from the *Griffin*'s furs to arrive.

The Montreal traders were now very jealous of La Salle. They had been angry when he built Fort Frontenac, and now that he was trading still farther west they were getting very few furs and they were furious. They sent men to Fort Brokenheart to kill La Salle. He escaped, but the *Griffin* never reached Fort Frontenac. Everyone felt sure that the Montreal traders had wrecked her.

This was a dreadful blow. La Salle's furs were gone, and with them the money for his exploration. It was winter; there was snow on the ground and ice on the rivers and lakes, but La Salle did not hesitate. He left his friend, Tonty of the Iron Hand, in charge of Fort Brokenheart. Then, with his faithful Iroquois servant, Nika, he snowshoed, walked, and waded a thousand miles back to Fort Frontenac. There he collected all the money he could get and returned to Fort Brokenheart.

LA SALLE LEAVING TONTY IN CHARGE

He found the fort empty, but Tonty safe with the Indians. Tonty had had a hand blown off in a battle and wore an iron hand in a glove. He had once struck an Indian lightly with it and the Indian fell down unconscious. After that the redmen said that Tonty had a devil in his glove, and they were careful never to anger him. La Salle now made ready for the trip down the Mississippi. In the spring they paddled off.

On April 6, after weeks of paddling, they reached the place where the Mississippi divides into three branches. La Salle, Tonty, and his friend Dautray each led canoes down a branch and met on the shore of the Gulf of Mexico. La Salle had done it! He took possession of the great south-west for Canada and France. He had made his dream come true.

But the story of La Salle doesn't end there. He tried to start a French settlement near the mouth of the Mississippi. But because he was a hard and stern leader, his men turned against him. One day he was murdered. It took other leaders to establish a French settlement there.

**5. The boy Kelsey discovered the prairies in 1690.**

Our next great explorer was Henry Kelsey, a lively, friendly boy of only nine years old when we first meet him. He had no home, and lived on what he could beg or steal in the streets of London. Then he got employment with the Hudson's Bay Company, and went to Fort Nelson.

Henry was a brave lad. The cold, bare land round Hudson Bay did not frighten him. The men kept him busy running errands while they made ready to trade with the Indians. When they arrived, Governor Geyer put on his gold-laced scarlet coat, plumed hat, and sword, and with a band playing before him went out to meet them. Henry was thrilled with the Indian chiefs in their painted robes and feathered head-dresses. When the speeches and exchanges of gifts were over, Henry would have liked to stay with them, but the Company's rule was strict: only the Governor and the chief trader were allowed to deal with the Indians.

But young Henry soon slipped out to play with the Indian boys. He learned their language and to shoot with bow and arrow. When the Governor heard this he scolded Kelsey. When that did not stop the boy, he thrashed him. Henry was now a tall lad and the thrashing angered him. When the Indians left, he climbed over the wall and went with them. He was gone for months. Then one day an Indian arrived with a letter for the Governor. Kelsey had written it on birch bark with a bit of charcoal and it said that if the Governor would let him return, he would bring many new tribes with their furs to Fort Nelson.

Governor Geyer was delighted to have new tribes to trade with and sent men to bring Kelsey in. The Governor forgave the young man and sent him out with the Assiniboines for the far-off Saskatchewan River. It was a long slow trip and Kelsey had many exciting adventures. They travelled 300 miles through the woods and then came out on the wide prairies. Henry was the first white man to see the buffalo roaming in great herds across the

HENRY KELSEY AND THE BEARS

plains. The men hunted, the women cooked, all feasted on buffalo meat as they moved west.

Kelsey's most exciting adventure came when, hunting with a friend, they met two bears which made for them. The Indian climbed a small tree, while Kelsey dashed into the brush. The bears followed the Indian and would have dragged him down had not Kelsey with a lucky shot killed one of them. The other turned against Kelsey, but could not find him, so went back to the Indian. Kelsey then dropped the second bear. After that the Indians named him the Little Giant.

By September, Kelsey and his Indians were in what we call the province of Saskatchewan. There they met the tribe called the Naywatamee Poets. Kelsey smoked the peace pipe with their chief and gave him a gold-laced coat, a musket, powder, shot, and tobacco. These fine things, he said, had been sent by the Great White Chief of the Bay, who invited the Indian chief to visit him in spring. The chief was pleased and promised to do so. The next summer Kelsey and his Indians went down with a great fleet of canoes full of furs to trade at Fort Nelson.

# 9 The French Canadians Fought the Iroquois and the English for Canada
## 1660 to 1700

### 1. The fight for Hudson Bay

Governor Frontenac managed the Iroquois well, but he quarrelled so often with his own men that the King ordered him to come home. Denonville, the new Governor, got on well with his own men, but got into trouble with the Iroquois.

His first adventure was a great success. The Hudson's Bay Company now had several trading posts on Hudson Bay. The Company's men were taking most of the northern furs from Canadian traders, so in 1670 Governor Denonville sent a party of voyageurs (canoemen) and Indians to attack them.

Among the voyageurs were three of the famous Le Moyne brothers. Seigneur Le Moyne had ten sons and every one of them grew up to play a brave part in Canada's fight for life. Pierre Le Moyne, Seigneur of Iberville, the greatest fighter of them all, was the real leader of this party. It was winter. They snowshoed through the forest from the Ottawa to the Abitibi River and paddled down to Moose Fort. It was a fearful trip, for

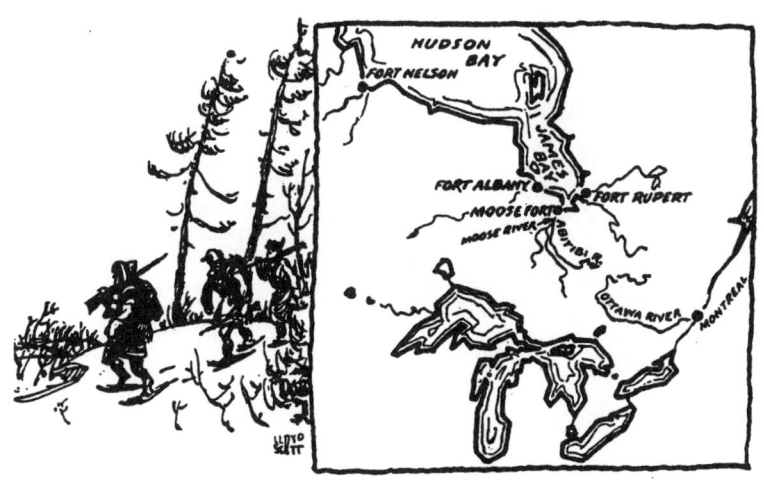

THE LE MOYNE BROTHERS AND WHERE THEY WENT

the woods were full of hungry wolves, and the river was full of ice cakes and whirlpools. It took them three months.

They camped on an island near Moose Fort. Then, just before dawn, they landed, crept up to the fort, and silently surrounded it. There they stood in amazement. There were no watchmen on the walls and the back gate was not locked. The three Le Moynes leaped the palisade and ran shouting to break down the house door. As they struck, it was opened by the English traders - in their night shirts, open-mouthed, still half asleep. A few shots were fired and the Canadians were masters of Moose Fort.

Leaving a few voyageurs to guard Moose Fort, the Canadians paddled swiftly across to Fort Charles, which had been renamed Fort Rupert. Again they found the English asleep and got in by a ladder. Someone dropped a grenade down the chimney, which wounded Mrs. Verner who was making breakfast. That wakened the men. They fought fiercely and Factor Verner held the house till the Canadians threatened to blow it up. Meantime, Iberville and his party had boarded an English ship at the dock, stamped on the deck to wake the crew, and captured them as they rushed up the stairs.

DE TROYES BURNING FORT RUPERT

De Troyes burned Fort Rupert and, loading the captured ship with the Company's furs, sailed back to Moose to pick up the ten cannon there. Iberville and his men raced the canoes back across James Bay to Fort Albany. They nearly drowned on the way for the huge ice cakes were grinding and plunging, but they boldly hoisted their canoes onto a big cake and, dragging them from cake to cake, got safely over.

When De Troyes reached Albany, he set up his guns and called on the Fort to surrender. Governor Sergeant refused, so De Troyes fired on it. Sergeant tried to get his men to go out to fight the Canadians, but they refused. They said they were not soldiers, but traders. If they lost their limbs, or were killed, the Company would not give them or their wives a pension, as the King did for his soldiers. Sergeant had to surrender. The Canadians had captured the Bay.

## 2. The wasp's nest

Next, Governor Denonville prepared to attack the Senecas, the Iroquois tribe which had been giving Canada the most trouble. He sent eight hundred French soldiers and four hundred Canadian volunteers to Fort Frontenac, and ordered the coureurs to round up as many Indians as possible to help them.

Coureurs Duluth and Durantaye came down the Great Lakes with two thousand western Indians, and a wild mob they were. But the coureurs were patient; they got them all to Lake Erie. Governor Denonville attacked the Senecas and won the battle. The Senecas fled and Denonville destroyed their town and burned all their wheat.

"The Governor has overturned a wasp's nest," said a Christian Iroquois. "Now he must kill the wasps or they will sting him."

And sting him they did, a terrible stinging! Indeed, poor young Canada was having a bad time. The war with the Iroquois had stopped the fur trade, so there was no money in the country. Small parties of Iroquois roamed among the Canadian villages, killing everyone they met. The farmers had to take refuge in the forts; there were no crops, the Canadians were starving.

At last Governor Denonville sent two Iroquois prisoners to ask their people to send men to a meeting to make peace. He promised that, if they did so, he would free all the Iroquois prisoners in Canada. The Iroquois agreed to do this, and peace might have been made if it had not been for the "Rat".

The Rat was a famous Huron chief who hated the Iroquois with a deadly hatred. The Governor had promised him that he would never stop fighting the Iroquois till they were destroyed. When the Rat heard that the Iroquois chiefs were coming to make peace with Canada, he made a plot to stop them. He and his friends lay in wait for the Iroquois, killed one of them, and seized the others. When they told the Rat that they had come to make peace, he told them that Denonville had sent him to kill them. He said he was sorry, and told them to go home, instead of to the peace meeting. The chiefs believed the

Rat and, when they got home, they told their tribes that Denonville was a wicked man who had planned to kill the Iroquois. He did not want to make peace at all, they said.

The Iroquois were furious. The "wasps" got ready to sting. Silently, one summer night, they surrounded the village of Lachine. At dawn they sprang upon the houses, killed two hundred people and carried off one hundred and twenty to be tortured. The news ran quickly up and down the river. All Canada trembled. Then a great cry went up for Frontenac.

"Give us Frontenac!" the Canadians cried to the King. "Give us Frontenac! Only he can save us." The King sent them Frontenac.

**3. The English won in Acadia in 1690.**

Frontenac was old now, but a great leader still. He knew that the Iroquois were getting their guns and ammunition from the English settlers. So he sent three war parties to attack part of New England. It was midwinter and the snow deep, but Canadians do not mind that. With their guns on their backs and their tobacco pipes swinging from cords round their necks, they marched briskly through the drifts. Each party attacked at night, caught the English settlers asleep, and killed and captured them as they rushed from their homes. The Canadians then burned their towns and marched home.

These cruel deeds roused the New Englanders to fury, and they prepared to attack Canada. In Boston, Sir William Phips gathered together seven ships and two hundred and eighty men, and led the New Englanders against Acadia. As the French Governor had only seventy men in Port Royal, he had to surrender the town. Phips left some of his soldiers to hold it, and returned to Boston.

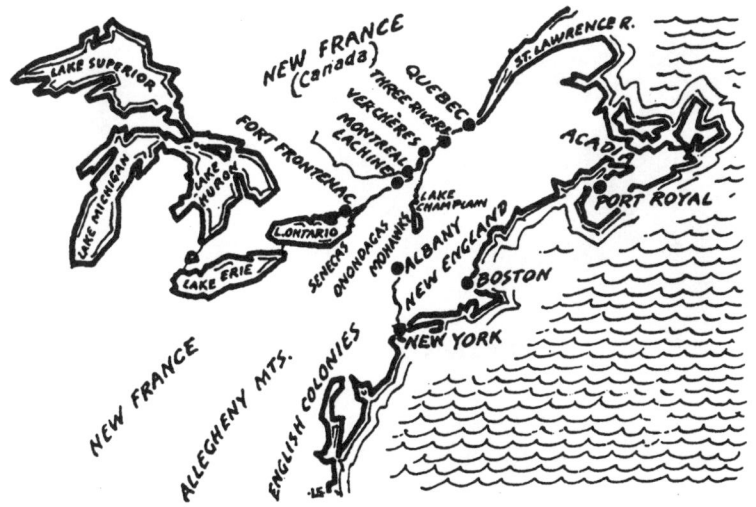

NEW ENGLAND AND NEW FRANCE

There he got ready to lead the attack on Quebec. The New Englanders collected thirty-two small ships, and twenty-two hundred farmers and fishermen for the fight, and sailed from Boston for the St. Lawrence.

**4. Frontenac saved Quebec for France.**

Frontenac had been warned that the English were preparing to attack Quebec, and he had spent the winter rebuilding the fort and making ready for the English attack. The great rock protected the town in front, but behind it the land slopes down to the St. Charles River, facing the Beauport shore. This was the danger point. Here Frontenac built a strong palisade with a deep ditch in front of it. All was ready when Phips anchored before the town. A boat brought an officer with a letter from Phips to Frontenac. The Canadians blindfolded him, and led him to Castle St. Louis.

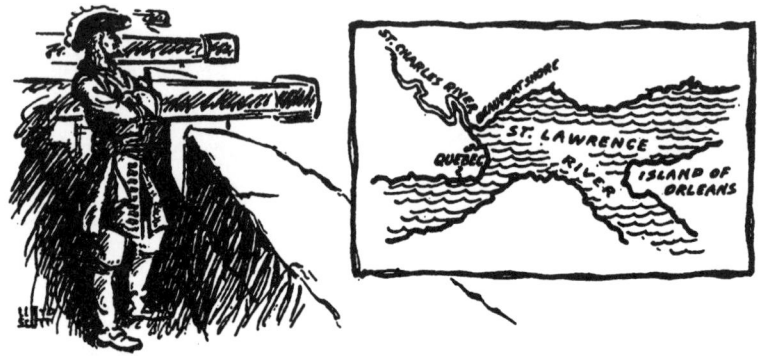

FRONTENAC AT QUEBEC

They took the bandage from his eyes and he saw a great room crowded with gentlemen in velvet and satin, gold lace and plumes. The Le Moynes were there and many another proud French Canadian. The English officer stared, then bowed to Frontenac and handed him the letter. It said that Phips had a large army and could easily take Quebec, but that to save life he would allow Frontenac to surrender if he did so within the hour.

This bold message made the proud old Governor angry. He swept the letter from the table with the point of his sword, and replied, "I will not keep you waiting so long! Tell your general that I will answer him through the mouth of my cannon."

As soon as he heard Frontenac's reply, Phips landed his men on the Beauport shore, from which they crossed the St. Charles River to attack Quebec from behind. The Le Moyne brothers met them with a band of sharpshooters who drove them back. The New Englanders were brave men; they came on again and again, dodging behind trees, fighting Indian-fashion, but at night they retreated to their boats. The next day the ships' cannon fired at the town, but many of the shots hit the cliff and did little damage.

The English ships had soon been so badly damaged by the Canadian cannon-balls that Phips took his men on board, and sailed his ships round behind the Island of Orleans for repairs. By the time they had been repaired, ice was forming in the river, and Phips had to hurry to get out of the river before he was frozen in.

## 5. The story of Madeleine of Vercheres

By this time the Iroquois had given up raiding the lower St. Lawrence. From Three Rivers downstream, the seigneuries were fairly safe, but those round Montreal lay right in the path of the Iroquois coming up the Richelieu. Farmers there went out in large parties, posted a guard, and then worked each man's fields in turn. At night they slept in the fort. Only now and then did they dare to return to their houses. Many a one who did so was killed, and many a brave story is told of bold fights and narrow escapes.

The bravest is the story of Madeleine of Vercheres. Her family's seigneury lay in the danger zone. The father was on duty in Quebec, the mother was in Montreal. The three children were at home where there was a strong blockhouse connected with the fort by a covered way.

One bright autumn morning the men were in the fields, the women and children, with two soldier guards, in the fort. Madeleine, who was fourteen, was at the landing watching a hired man fish when they heard firing in the fields. "Run, Mademoiselle, run!" shouted the man and, with bullets whistling about their ears, they ran together for the gate. Dashing through it, they barred it in the faces of forty Iroquois.

"To arms!" shouted Madeleine, but the soldiers had disappeared and the women were crying for their

71

MADELEINE VERCHÈRES AND THE IROQUOIS

husbands who were at work in the fields. Madeleine hurried the women to a safe place behind the palisade. In the blockhouse with the ammunition she found the two soldiers, one hiding, the other with a lighted match in his hand.

"What are you doing with that match?" cried Madeleine.

"Lighting the powder to blow us up," he replied.

"You are cowards," said the girl, driving them out. "We must fight to the death." Then, snatching up guns, she and her two younger brothers and the two soldiers began firing from the loopholes in the blockhouse walls.

The Iroquois, who did not know how many soldiers there were in the fort, were now tomahawking the men in the fields. A canoe dashed up to the landing with the Fontaine family, who were trying to reach the fort. The soldiers dared not go down with their guns to guard them, so Madeleine went herself and led them safely in.

Night brought a snow-storm, but the Iroquois still lurked about. Madeleine gathered her troops, seven persons. She sent Fontaine with the two soldiers to the blockhouse to guard the women and children, while she, her brothers, and an old man of eighty manned the four bastions. All night in the storm the brave four kept firing their guns, while shouts of "All's well" rang from fort to blockhouse and back again. In the morning Madame Fontaine begged her husband to take them to a stronger fort, but he refused to leave the children.

"We must never give up the fort," said Madeleine. "If the Iroquois take one of our forts, they will think they can take others and grow bolder than ever."

The Iroquois did not again attack the fort, but they hung around for a week. By that time the Governor of Montreal had sent a lieutenant with forty men to protect the Canadians. Madeleine was dozing with her head on a table and her gun across her arms when one of the sentinels heard a sound from the river. He woke Madeleine, who called "Who are you?"

"Frenchmen!" was the answer. Madeleine hurried to the landing where she saluted the lieutenant.

"Monsieur, I surrender my arms to you," she said.

"They are in good hands, Mademoiselle," he replied.

"Better than you think, sir," said Madeleine proudly as she led him to inspect her little army, with every man at his post.

# 10 Peace and War: Good Times and Hard Times
### 1700 to 1760

## 1. The Canadians enjoyed themselves.

Now that the war was over and the Iroquois had made peace, the Canadians could live comfortably. New settlers came in and the St. Lawrence began to look like a long street with a row of houses and churches on both sides.

The houses were made of log or stone with the living-room and its big fire-place in the middle, the kitchen on one side, and the bedroom on the other. The older children slept in the attic. The Canadians made their own furniture. There was no electric light in those days; a few people made candles of tallow, but most families went to bed at dark, or worked by the light of the fire. Behind the house stood the barn and stables, and round it were the outdoor oven, the soap-making kettle, and the meat-smoking house.

All these people were farmers, so there was no sale for grain or vegetables; each family grew what it needed. This took only a few acres on the river end of their long, narrow farms, and left the back acres in woods where their cows, pigs, and sheep fed. There, too, they shot rabbits and deer for meat, and foxes, wolves, and bears for skins to make clothes and boots. The women spun and wove their woollen clothes. The French Canadians had no tea or coffee, but drank milk or beer. They grew their own tobacco. They were called habitants, the French word meaning inhabitants.

The church was the community centre where everyone went every Sunday. The curé (priest) was their best friend. He preached to them, listened to all their troubles, and advised them what to do. The captain of militia was their next best friend. They chose him and he reported their wishes to the Governor and Council in Quebec. He brought back the Government's orders and all the latest news, and read them out to the people on Sunday after church. They all listened carefully and went home talking over what they had heard.

Their seigneur (lord) was their magistrate (judge), but he could only judge and punish them for small crimes; for big ones the accused person had to go before the Governor in Quebec. Most seigneurs were kind to their habitants.

PRIEST       MILITIA OFFICER   MILITIAMAN

## 2. The Verendryes led Canada out across the prairies.

Pierre La Verendrye's father was the Governor of Three Rivers. So Pierre and his nine brothers and sisters lived in the old stone fort with its thick walls with loopholes to shoot through when the Iroquois attacked. There they listened to the exciting stories that the fur traders told about the west. Pierre decided that when he grew up he would explore that far-off land, but he was married and had four sons before he got a chance to do so.

Then the Governor made him commander of the trading post at Nipigon. One day Ochagach, an old Indian, came in with his furs and told Verendrye a wonderful story. He said that farther west there was a big lake that had a river flowing out of it towards the west.

"I paddled down that river," said Ochagach, "till I came to the sea. There I saw large towns where ships came to trade."

Verendrye knew that the Spaniards had towns on the Pacific shore of Mexico, so he thought Ochagach must have reached the Pacific Ocean. The Indian drew Verendrye a map and he hurried down to Quebec to ask the Governor for the men, canoes, and food he needed to follow Ochagach's river to the Pacific. The Governor refused to give him supplies, but gave him a monopoly of the fur trade in any new land that he found.

"I will build a trading post," thought Verendrye, "and trade there till I get enough furs to pay for building another post farther west. I will build post after post, each farther west than the last, till I get to the Pacific. It will be hard work, but I can do it." He almost did do it.

It took all of Verendrye's money to buy canoes and supplies and to hire fifty voyageurs. He promised to pay the merchants with furs for goods to trade, and they filled

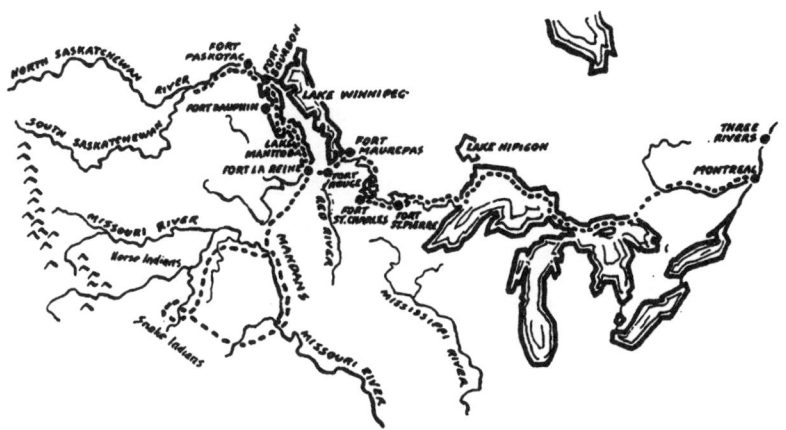

THE VÉRENDRYES' JOURNEY ACROSS THE PRAIRIES

his canoes with guns, knives, hatchets, coloured cloth, beads, and tobacco. He took with him his sons, Jean, Pierre, Francois, and his nephew Jemeraye. The whole town came down to see them off. The priest prayed for a safe voyage; the voyageurs in their bright red shirts and sashes stepped down into the canoes; the women cried; the men cheered; the paddles fell; they were off for the Pacific.

By fall they were in the woods north of Lake Superior. Verendrye built a post and traded there, while Jemeraye with twenty-five men paddled west up the wild rivers and built Fort St. Pierre on Rainy Lake. Building post after post, they worked their way west to Lake Winnipeg where they built Fort Rouge (Winnipeg), and Fort La Reine (Portage la Prairie) where crowds of Assiniboines came to trade.

The Assiniboines took Verendrye south to visit the Mandans, who lived in large, clean houses in neat towns. The Mandans told him about the white men who lived beyond the mountains on the sea-shore. This was very exciting news. Verendrye was ill when the news came and had to return to Canada, but he sent Pierre and Francois west to question the Horse Indians. This tribe sent the boys on to the Bows.

"We are going to fight the Snake Indians," said the Bows. "If you come with us you will see the shining mountains. From their tops you can see the sea."

The brothers went with them, and on New Year's Day saw, far away in the west, a long line of shining white peaks: the Rocky Mountains. The Verendrye boys begged for a guide to lead them through the mountains, but no one would go. So they hurried back to Fort La Reine to tell their father of their discovery and to send to Canada for supplies for a trip through the mountains to the sea.

Meanwhile Francois had discovered Lake Manitoba, and his father had sent him to explore that lake for a river flowing from the west. He got into the Saskatchewan and paddled west up that great river as far as the forks where the North Saskatchewan and the South Saskatchewan join. Either branch would have carried him to the mountains, but he did not know that. He built Fort Paskoyac (The Pas), traded there, and took his furs down to Fort La Reine.

He arrived there to find that the Montreal men were again refusing to send them supplies. Father and sons returned to Canada together and Verendrye made peace with the merchants. The Verendryes were ready to start for the west again when Verendrye died. His sons begged to go back to the west to finish their exploration, but the new Governor did not favour these brave young men. It was fifty years before a Canadian explorer reached the Pacific.

**3. The Newfoundlanders got a Governor.**

Peace brought good times to the Newfoundlanders, too. The farmers now could plough their fields and plant their crops without being shot at by Indians or French soldiers.

IN THE STOCKS

The fishermen brought in twice as many fish as before, and trade increased greatly. At last the Newfoundlanders had something besides fish to eat; also they now had blankets for their beds, and new clothes. Ships brought salt beef, pork, bacon, and butter from Ireland; wool from England; linen from France; iron from Spain; and fresh meat, corn, and flour from New England.

All these years the Newfoundlanders had been begging England to send them a Governor and now at last she did so. Governor Osborne was an honest man and a hard worker. He divided the island into districts and appointed a magistrate (judge) for each district. He built a court house and a prison in St. John's and prisons in several other places. He also set up stocks in the towns, so that the magistrates could punish people who had committed small crimes by making them sit in them.

At first the magistrates had a hard time. The people had suffered so much from the Fishing Admirals that they now resented having anyone over them, and they sometimes attacked the magistrates. Also, the Fishing Admirals kept interfering with the magistrates. But after a few years the Admirals gave up trying to rule the island. The people learned to obey the laws, and Newfoundland became a proper colony.

## 4. The English built Halifax.

Now that England had won Acadia, the English Government appointed a Committee to start a colony there. The Committee offered land to any soldier who would go to Acadia, and promised to take the colonists to Nova Scotia free and to feed them there for a year. It was a good offer and over two thousand settlers accepted it. The King appointed Edward Cornwallis Governor of the colony, and the settlers sailed in thirteen ships. They reached Chebucto Harbour early in July, and canoes full of Indians paddled out to welcome them. Chebucto is one of the three largest and safest harbours in the world, and there is good fishing near it. The land round it is rocky but well wooded.

Governor Cornwallis soon had the settlers cutting down trees to clear land for their houses and to make logs to build them. As soon as there was a clear space, Engineer Bruce laid out the town with straight streets. A steep round hill behind the town was set aside for a fort.

By the time the colonists had built the fort and church, Engineer Bruce had divided the centre of the town into lots, one to be given to each family. So that the lots would be given out fairly, the Council gave each lot a number, and then prepared papers each with the number of a lot on it. The papers were put into a hat, and the head of each family drew one. Then one man drew for each four bachelors. Mr. Bruce gave the lots to those who had drawn their numbers. The day of the drawing was Nova Scotia's first holiday. There were races, games, and a picnic with food from the ship. After that, each family worked on its own house and garden.

DRAWING LOTS FOR LAND

## 5. Governor Lawrence exiled the Acadians.

The first English Governors of Nova Scotia had been kind to the Acadians. The Governors had needed the food the Acadians grew, and when they did not take the oath of loyalty to the King of England, the Governors did not punish them.

But now England and France were beginning to fight a really big war. They were fighting to see which one would be the top dog in Europe, in Asia, and in America. The Governor of Nova Scotia, Governor Lawrence, was a soldier. When he gave an order, he expected it to be obeyed. He ordered the Acadians to take the oath. When they did not do so, he ordered his men to round them all up and send them out of the province.

The Acadians in Grand Pre were to be sent away by ship. Colonel Winslow, the officer in charge there, had his men camp round the church and help the Acadians cut their grain and take in the crop while he waited for the ships to come. Then one day three ships sailed into the harbour. Winslow ordered all the fathers of families to gather in the church. Over four hundred men came. Suddenly guards with guns sprang up at the doors and

THE ACADIANS GO INTO EXILE

windows. Colonel Winslow and his officers entered and Winslow told the men that he had been sent to take them away. He was sorry, but he had to obey his orders. Each morning he let twenty men go to spend the day with their families, and they returned with food and loving messages for the others.

At last more carrier ships came. The Acadians marched down to them, carrying their children and the little bundles containing the few possessions they were allowed to take with them. About two thousand people sailed from Grand Pre. Altogether more than six thousand Acadians were torn away from their happy homes and driven into far countries where they did not know anyone. Many died. Most of the others lived, poor and sad. Very few did well. In the end they were allowed to return, as you shall hear.

**6. How the British won Canada.**

Britain and France had now been fighting their top-dog war for over sixty years. All those years the French Canadians had been fighting the English settlers in small wars. England now had a large navy to carry her soldiers across the ocean to America, so she was ready to fight it out with France for Canada.

CANADA, AND BRITAIN'S THIRTEEN COLONIES

The English settlers were ready to help Britain. So many English colonists had come out that, besides Newfoundland and Acadia, the English now had thirteen colonies along the Atlantic coast. The colonists were farmers, fishermen, and merchants, and they had already taken up most of the good land between the Atlantic Ocean and the Allegheny Mountains. They were beginning to move over into the land between the mountains and the Mississippi River. This land, you remember, had been explored by the Canadians, so they got ready to fight. They strengthened their old trading posts and forts, and built new ones where they won several battles.

France could not send many soldiers to help the Canadians, because her ships could not get past the big English fleet in the Atlantic. But she did send them a good leader, a great soldier called General Montcalm. He found Canada in great trouble. Intendant Bigot was a very bad man. He and his friends took the people's grain and furs, sold them, and used the money to buy liquor and give wild parties for their friends. Montcalm stopped all that. He called every man able to fight into the army and he led them so well that for the first two years the Canadians won all the battles.

The Canadians won these battles partly because the English had no good leaders. At last William Pitt became the leader in England. He sent good men to lead the English settlers, and they soon began to win battles. Pitt sent a large army under young General James Wolfe to take Quebec. Wolfe saw at once that he could not take Quebec from the front. The only way would be to find a path leading up to the top of the rock, get his men up there, and attack the cliff on level ground. The British looked and looked, but for weeks no path could be found. Wolfe fell sick with worry, for the summer was passing and he knew that he would have to leave before the river froze.

Barely in time, someone found a steep path up through a narrow gorge west of the city. Wolfe sent a strong force to attack Quebec on the east side. While Montcalm and his men fought on the east, Wolfe took most of his soldiers in the night up the river to the west, where they landed and climbed the path. In the morning when Montcalm returned from the eastside battle, he found Wolfe and his men lined up ready to fight on the "Plains of Abraham", Abraham Martin's old farm. Montcalm and his men rushed out through the gates to

THE TAKING OF QUEBEC

defend Quebec and Canada. They fought bravely, but the English won. Montcalm and Wolfe were both killed. They were brave men and good soldiers; all Canadians are proud of them. One monument to them both stands in the Governor's Garden. You will see it when you go to Quebec.

Quebec surrendered on September 18, and the French Governor of Canada and his troops retired to Montreal. The St. Lawrence was freezing, so the British army had to wait nearly a year before it could move up the river. The next summer three British armies surrounded Montreal and the last French Governor surrendered Canada to the British.

# 11 The French and the English Got On Well Together
### 1763 to 1795

**1. In Quebec they helped each other.**

Their first winter under English rule was a hard one for the French Canadians. They were short of everything, but they were thankful that the fighting was over. The King of England appointed three English officers to rule Canada until the peace treaty could be signed. General Murray ruled in Quebec, General Gage in Three Rivers, and General Haldimand in Montreal. All three spoke French. They were sorry for the Canadians, and helped them in every way they could.

In Quebec, General Murray found that the farmers had been fighting and had not got their crops in. He sent his English soldiers to help them. The French Canadians were poor, but they invited the Englishmen into their homes and gave them good dinners and parties. When the Canadians' food gave out, the soldiers shared their rations with them.

When Murray and the other two generals had any business to do with the habitants, they did it with their French captains of militia. The captains explained it to the people after church on Sundays. Also the three generals made the captains of militia magistrates (judges) so that they could try criminals in French and by their own French law. All this kindness made the French Canadians like the British.

## 2. The Governor called the Acadians home.

In Acadia, the English Governor sent out word that the Acadians could now come home if they liked. They had been away for eight years. Some of them had settled in New England or in Canada, but many were far away in the West Indies, or Louisiana. Far or near, they all heard that call and many of them started at once for home. Most of them were poor. They had to walk hundreds of miles; some walked a thousand miles or more. The journey took them months, even years. Many died on the way, but a good many reached home safely. Their old farms had been given to others, but the Governor gave the Acadians new ones in the St. John River country and their children live there to this day.

THE ACADIANS RETURN FROM EXILE

Other Acadians settled in Isle St. Jean, which the English named Prince Edward Island. The King made Walter Patterson their Governor. In the spring, 220 British families arrived, and Governor Patterson gave them each a large lot to build a house on and twelve acres of pasture for their cattle. The town was laid out with wide streets, and land was left for a church and market. The settlers called it Charlottetown after the Queen of England. The new farmers planted wheat, corn, oats, and barley. The wheat did not grow well, but the other grains did. The potatoes grew amazingly. One man planted three bushels, and in the fall dug up 160 bushels. The Island is still famous for its fine potatoes.

Now that Nova Scotia belonged to England for good, the New Englanders began moving into it. James Simonds and James White, two young men from Maine, opened the first store in Saint John. New Englanders were taking up land up the Saint John River and they had nowhere to shop, so the two young fellows thought Saint John would be a good place to start.

They bought a small ship and loaded it with goods, frames for their houses, and twenty settlers. They were all young and willing to work hard. In two days the young men had set up their houses, their wives had unpacked, and "Simonds and White" were keeping store on the deck of the ship. Customers swarmed round them. While the young owners worked like beavers to serve them, the settlers helped to unload the ship so that she could be sent back to fetch more goods.

Next, a large party of Scots arrived in a leaky old ship called the *Hector*. They were poor people and had not brought enough food to last through the six weeks' voyage from Scotland. Nearly everyone was sick and many had died on the way. The Indians tried to scare the

THE PIPER LEADS THE SCOTS ASHORE FROM THE *Hector*

Scots. They dressed up in their wildest paint and feathers and marched to the beach with guns, tomahawks, and war-whoops ready. But the Scots were Highlanders, big men in kilts. They waded ashore led by their pipers playing the bagpipes. The Indians had never heard bagpipes before, and the strange, wild music terrified them. They fled to the woods and never afterwards dared to attack the Scots.

## 3. French and British Canadians became partners in the fur trade.

Alexander Henry lived in Albany, the centre of the British fur trade. He was twenty-one and already a clever trader. When the British soldiers were fighting to take Montreal, he loaded a canoe with goods and paddled down the Richelieu River to trade with the troops. His canoe was wrecked, but he swam to shore.

Old Seigneur Leduc found him and took him to his manor house. Leduc had been a coureur. He told young Henry such wonderful stories of the Canadian fur trade in the west that Henry hired Campion, a Canadian trader, to guide him to Mackinac. While Campion collected canoes and hired voyageurs, Henry hurried back to Albany to buy goods to trade.

ALEXANDER HENRY HIDING FROM THE INDIANS

When all was ready they paddled up the Champlain Trail. They were near Mackinac when they heard that Chief Pontiac of Detroit was stirring up the Indians of the north-west and that they were killing every Englishman they could catch. Campion made Henry change clothes with him. When they reached the trading post, Campion acted as the trader and Henry as one of his voyageurs. Henry took a room in a house and hid there, but some one told on him. The Indians forced their way in and demanded his trade goods. Henry was terribly frightened, but he refused. Luckily that very day three hundred British soldiers marched into Mackinac and the Indians left.

In the spring Henry went up to Sault Ste. Marie where Cadotte, a French Canadian with an Indian wife, was trading. Henry stayed all summer with Cadotte who told him many things about the Canadian fur trade, and Madame Cadotte taught him to speak Chipewyan. That fall Sault Ste. Marie burned down. The people had to live on fish till the lake froze and they could return to Mackinac. There, Wawatam, a Chipewyan, took a great fancy to Henry and adopted him as a brother.

Being adopted was a fortunate thing for Henry, for Chief Pontiac was now on the warpath. Henry was in Mackinac when the Indians who favoured Pontiac seized the fort. They did it by a trick. It was the King's birthday, a holiday, and the Indians invited the English soldiers to come out of the fort to watch their lacrosse match. The English did so. Suddenly the ball flew over the wall into the fort. Indians and squaws rushed in after it. Once inside, the squaws snatched guns from under their blankets and gave them to their men, who killed most of the white men and took possession of the fort.

Henry was not at the lacrosse match, but the Indians seized him and fourteen other white men. They crowded them into a hut, and tied each by the neck to the centre pole. The red men then danced around, shouting that they were going to kill and eat them. They were preparing to do this when Wawatam arrived. He bought Henry from them, disguised him as an Indian, and hid him in his own camp.

The Indians killed most of their prisoners and they kept hunting for Henry. So, in the spring, he went back to the Sault where he hid for weeks in Cadottes's attic. At last a canoe arrived with Indians from Niagara. They brought a wampum belt from Sir William Johnson, an Irishman who had married a beautiful Indian girl and who was a leader among the Iroquois. The Niagara Indians told the Chipewyans that the war was over, and invited them to come down to Niagara.

"There," they said, "Sir William has his kettles ready and his fires lit for a great feast."

"You had better come," they said, "for the British are coming with a great army of white warriors."

When the western tribes heard this, they agreed to go down to the peace feast. The Indians now made much of

Henry and took him with them to Niagara. From there, Henry went on to Montreal to begin business. He and Cadotte had become partners; Cadotte in the west was to collect the furs and send them to Henry in Montreal. Henry was to ship them to England, sell them, buy goods to trade, and send the trade goods to Cadotte at Mackinac. They made so much money working together in this way that other teams of French Canadian traders and English Canadian merchants became partners. You will read many exciting stories about these French-English Canadian partners.

**4. English sailors explored Canada's west coast.**

Now that Britain owned Canada she sent Captain Cook to explore our west coast. James Cook was a poor English boy who got a job on a ship and worked and studied till he got his certificate as a mate. He was on one of Wolfe's ships at the capture of Quebec. After that he measured the different depths of the St. Lawrence from Quebec to the sea, and made a chart to show the shallow places where ships might be wrecked. He explored the coasts of New Zealand and Australia, and was then sent to search for the North-West Passage. By the time he had sailed across the Pacific from Australia his ships needed repairs, so he anchored in Nootka Sound to work on them. No one knew then that there was a Vancouver Island; Cook thought he had reached the mainland. His ships had hardly anchored before a fleet of canoes full of Indians dashed out from the land to surround them. The chief stood up in his canoe, threw out handfuls of feathers and made a long speech. He and his Indians were painted in bright colours. They wore cedar-bark cloaks, and had head-dresses shaped like the heads of birds or animals.

CAPTAIN COOK TRADING WITH THE INDIANS

They did not go on board the ships, but made the white men understand that they wanted to trade.

The next day hundreds of Indians appeared and swarmed over the ships. They traded their cedar-bark cloaks and rich black sea-otter skins for knives, buttons, copper or tin mugs, cans, kettles, and any bit of brass the sailors had or could find for them. The men stripped the ship and themselves of every piece of metal they had, for they knew that these beauiful skins were valuable.

While his men repaired the ships, Captain Cook visited the Indians, who were friendly enough, but were inclined to steal if they got a chance. Their houses were large, built of planks, and had totem poles set before them. The houses were furnished with large carved chests in which the Indians kept their skins, their mats, and the carved masks they wore at their ceremonies. The men hunted, fished, and built canoes from the trunks of huge trees. The women cleaned the fish and preserved them by drying and smoking them.

When his ships were repaired, Cook sailed for Alaska. On his way north he explored several of the beautiful inlets that run many miles back into the land. The one we call Cook's Inlet was so large that Cook hoped it might lead through to Hudson Bay, but after he

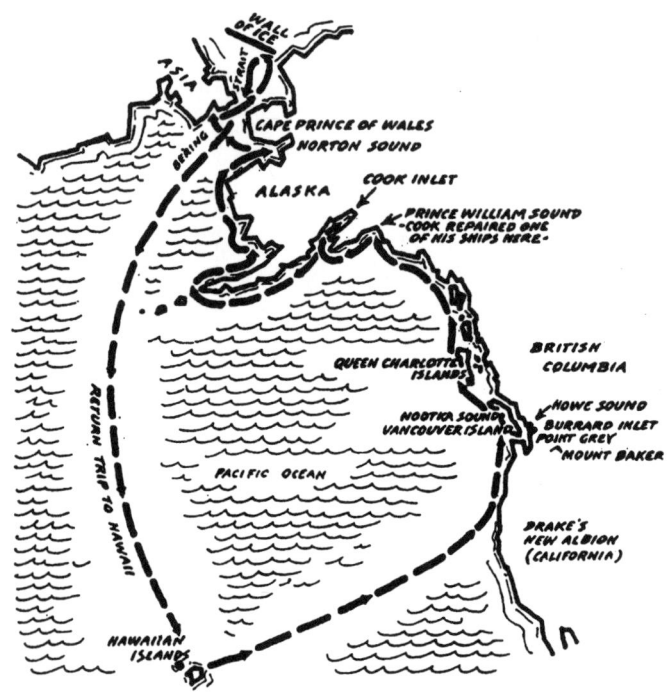

CAPTAIN COOK'S VOYAGE ALONG THE WEST COAST

and his men had sailed through Bering Strait, they were stopped by the ice. Cook returned to the Hawaiian Islands for the winter. He was killed there in a scuffle with some natives.

Captain Cook's ships stopped in China on the way home, and the sailors found the rich Chinese willing to pay big prices for the otter skins they had bought from the North American natives. News quickly spread that furs from our west coast could be bought cheaply and sold at a great profit, and trading ships soon came. Captain Meares reached Nootka first. He bargained with Chief Maquinna for some land, and built a trading post and a ship to collect furs.

Meares was just well started in business when two Spanish ships sailed into his "Friendly Cove". The Spanish commander declared that all this coast belonged to Spain. He seized Meares' ships and imprisoned Meares and his men. When England heard this, she was angry and for a while it looked as if she might fight Spain. Instead they held a meeting, and agreed that the west coast fur trade should be free to all nations.

Britain then sent Captain George Vancouver to Nootka to take back Meares' property, to make charts of the west coast, and to search for the North-West Passage. Britain gave him two small ships, and he sailed from England round the south of Africa and across the Indian and Pacific Oceans to America.

It was spring when they arrived and Vancouver decided to use the good summer weather for charting the coast, and to return to Nootka in the fall to take back Meares' property. So they started up the coast, sailing patiently in and out of hundreds of little bays and long inlets. Vancouver named Point Grey, Burrard Inlet, Howe Sound, Mount Baker, and other places after the men of his crew. Botanist Archie Menzies made notes of the trees, plants, and animals. The sailors were careful to treat the Indians politely and they, in turn, brought fish, meat, and drinking water to the ships.

In August, Vancouver turned south to Nootka to take over Meares' property from the Spanish commander Don Quadra. The sailors rested; the Indians entertained them; Vancouver and Don Quadra argued politely about the property and politely disagreed. So in October Vancouver took his ships to Hawaii for the winter. He spent the second summer exploring the Queen Charlotte Islands, and the third on the coast of Alaska. Vancouver did not find the North-West Passage, but his maps and charts are still used by those who sail these waters.

# 12     The United Empire Loyalists Came To Canada
### 1775 to 1840

**1. The English colonies became the United States.**

Britain had sent soldiers to fight to protect the English colonists against the French Canadians. These soldiers had won the war and Canada now belonged to Britain. The Canadians could not fight against the English colonies any more, so the colonies were safe. But the war had cost Britain a lot of money, and she said that the English colonists must help to pay for it. The colonists refused to pay; instead they fought what is known as the American War of Independence against Britain. They won that war, and formed a new nation called the United States.

But the people in the United States had come from Britain. They were British, and many of them had refused to fight against their motherland. Because they were loyal to Britain and to the British Empire, these people were called Loyalists. The fighting party treated the Loyalists very cruelly. They beat them, burned their houses, imprisoned them, even killed some of them. Thomas Hooper was a Loyalist. His neigbours stole his cattle and pigs, and robbed his house. While Hooper was away, they took the bed from under his sick wife and left her lying on the bare floor of a shed till she died.

2. **The Loyalists went to Nova Scotia and Prince Edward Island, and made the new province of New Brunswick.**

The British were sorry for the Loyalists, and they offered to carry them to the West Indies or to Canada, and to give them land there. Most of them came to Canada. Britain told all the Loyalists who wished to go to Canada to gather in New York, and she appointed Governor Carleton to take them north. Sir Guy Carleton chose Brook Watson to collect ships and food for the voyages.

Brook had been a homeless boy so he worked hard for the Loyalists. Whenever Sir Guy had Loyalists ready to sail to Nova Scotia, Watson had ships and supplies of food ready to carry them there. Nine ships took five hundred to Annapolis, Nova Scotia, a village with only

ON GUARD BEFORE FORT ANNE AT OLD PORT ROYAL (NOW ANNAPOLIS ROYAL)

one hundred people. Every Annapolis family took in as many as it could. The rest of the women and children filled the churches and the army barracks. The men and boys camped in the streets.

By the next spring Nova Scotia was well filled up with Loyalists, so Carleton and Watson began sending them to Saint John. It was a cold, wet spring and the Loyalists shivered as they looked at their new home. But they soon warmed up rushing around looking for their lots and cutting down trees to build their homes. By Christmas, Saint John was a real city with ten thousand people. It was the first real city in Canada.

Next, a band from New Jersey came to Saint John. The city was so full that several of the new families took a boat up the river to Fredericton. They found a few Loyalists there already. They were living in tents, and feeling very wet, cold, and sad. It was too late to build; they had to live in tents all winter. When the snow began to fall, they expected to freeze to death, but the snow kept falling, thick and soft, till it almost buried their tents. Instead of freezing them, it was like a thick blanket that helped to keep them warm.

LOYALISTS BUILDING THEIR NEW HOMES IN CANADA

Spring came at last and the families began to build log houses. It was hard work, for they had very few axes to cut and trim the logs and no bricks to make chimneys. But the men got the logs up and roofed the houses with poles which they covered with bark. The boys and girls brought heaps of moss and helped the women to stuff it into the cracks between the logs. Then they collected stones for the men to build stone fire-places for heating and cooking. By fall they all had houses and little patches of potatoes.

Thomas Hooper moved his family to Prince Edward Island. The Islanders now had good farms and they were also making good money out of the sea-cow fishery. The sea-cow is a large whale-like animal, valuable for its oil. Sea-cows swarmed on Prince Edward Island's shores. The fishermen killed so many that it looked as if they would all be killed. That would have been a great loss, so the Assembly made a law which said that each fisherman could kill only a certain number.

## 3. Governor Haldimand helped the Loyalists in Quebec.

While the Loyalists were settling in the provinces of eastern Canada, they were also pouring into Quebec. That was nearer for them than Nova Scotia. To reach Quebec they had only to tramp through the woods from Maine or New York, or take a canoe or boat down the Richelieu River. But it was a hard trek and they could carry little, so most of them reached Canada worn out and starving. Governor Haldimand had blankets, wood, and food stored for them in the villages along the St. Lawrence. The Canadians sheltered as many as they could in their homes, till the Governor could get them placed on farms of their own.

Aunt Hannah Hemstreet and her two sons walked to Canada. Uncle John had been shot by the American colonists, so the family fled. James and George were twins, big strong fellows, fifteen years old. Luckily Aunt Hannah was a little woman; when she got too tired to walk farther, the boys carried her. Sometimes they made a chair for her; sometimes each in turn carried her on his back for a while. Their food gave out and they dared not shoot for fear of being heard and caught, but George managed to snare several rabbits and they reached Canada safely.

**4. The Loyalists started Ontario.**

Sir William Johnson, a handsome Irishman, opened a store in the country of the Mohawks (an Iroquois tribe), who lived south-east of Lake Ontario. Then he married beautiful Molly Brant, their chief's daughter. The Mohawks liked Johnson so much that when the English colonists fought the War of Independence against Britain, he was able to keep them on Britain's side. The Mohawks moved to Canada, where they made the first big Loyalist settlement in Ontario. Britain gave them land beside the

LOYALISTS SAILING DOWN THE RICHELIEU RIVER TO CANADA

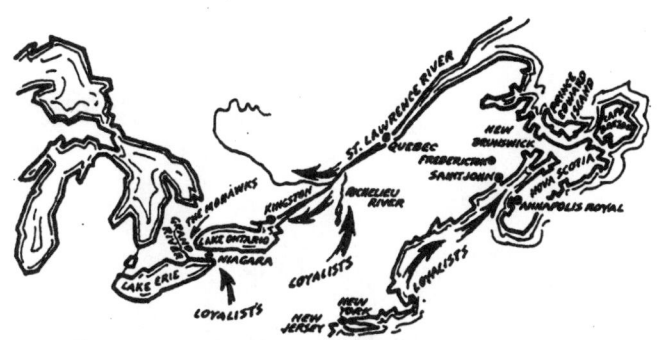

ROUTES BY WHICH THE LOYALISTS REACHED CANADA

Grand River. There they had a sawmill, a grist mill, a school, and a church. The church was the first one in Ontario, and the Indians also used it for Council meetings and tribal dances. The Mohawks still live by Grand River, and they still use the church.

Captain Michael Grass led the next group of Loyalists to Ontario. The party rowed up the St. Lawrence to Fort Frontenac in open boats with five or six families crowded into each. When the boats reached a rapid, four men remained in each one to guide it with poles, while all the others walked along the shore, pulling the boat along by a rope. The hot sun blazed down on them and they had to drink the river water; many of the children were sick and several died. When they reached Frontenac, which they renamed Kingston, everyone went to work to get a log house built before winter. It was too late to sow grain, but Captain Grass had the Government send up turnip seed which he divided among them. Each family dug a little garden, sowed it, and after the first frost harvested a good crop of turnips.

## 5. The Canadians began to govern themselves.

The French Canadians had always been governed by the King of France. You remember that he sent out a Governor, a Bishop, and an Intendant to rule Canada.

LOYALISTS ELECTING MEMBERS TO AN ASSEMBLY

They chose a number of Canadians to form a Council to advise them and together they made up the Government. The settlers themselves had nothing to do with it. They had their captains of militia who told the Governor and Council what the people wanted, but the captains had no power to make the Governor and Council do what the people wanted. The French in France were governed in this way, so the French Canadians were used to it and did not mind it.

But the white Loyalists were English. In each English colony, you remember, there was a Governor and Council, and an Assembly which the people elected to vote on their laws. When the Loyalists came to Canada they wanted to elect an Assembly to make their laws as they had done at home. Nova Scotia, New Brunswick, and Prince Edward Island all elected Assemblies. Newfoundland had had one years before, but it had been taken from her. She was now working to get it back. The Loyalists in Quebec and most of the French Canadians there wanted to elect one, so England divided the big province of Canada into two provinces, Quebec and Ontario, and gave them each an Assembly.

She then joined all the provinces, but not Newfoundland, together in one country called British North America, and made Sir Guy Carleton its Governor-General. The different provinces did not know or care much about one another then, but at least the parts of our country were brought together under one name. This was the beginning of making our provinces into one country.

# 13 The Canadians Won the Relay Race to the Pacific Ocean
### 1750 to 1810

**1. Anthony Henday carried the baton to Alberta.**

You remember how the King of France sent Jacques Cartier to find a way through Canada to the Pacific? That way turned out to be a very long one. It was so long that it became a relay race with different men running different parts of it. Cartier carried the baton as far west as Montreal; Champlain carried it on to Lake Huron, Radisson and Groseilliers to Lake Superior, the Verendryes to Manitoba, Henry Kelsey to Saskatchewan.

Anthony Henday carried it to Alberta. Anthony was an English boy who had fallen in with smugglers who smuggled silks and brandy from France into England. One night the police caught them. Anthony escaped, but the officers had seen him and he was outlawed. That meant that if they caught him, he would be hanged. He hid in London, but was always in danger. He was glad when he got a job with the Hudson's Bay Company and was sent out to York Factory.

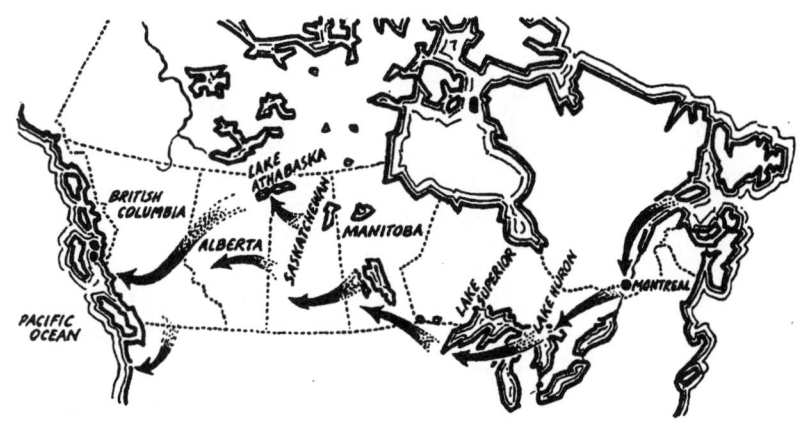

THE RELAY RACE ACROSS CANADA

Henday worked hard for the Company, but he was young and life in the Fort was dull. Like Kelsey, Anthony longed to be off hunting with the Indians. The Verendryes had gone, but their trading posts up the Saskatchewan were getting most of the furs, and trade at Hudson Bay was poor.

That summer a band of Assiniboines paddled down the Hayes River and camped outside York Factory. While the Governor held a council with the chiefs, the braves lay about, smoking; the squaws stirred the cooking pots hung over the fires; the children and dogs raced and played. For a while Anthony watched them all; then he slipped out to visit them. He asked them so many questions about their country that Big Elk laughed and said it would be easier to take him to their country than to answer all his questions. Henday was delighted. The Governor gave him permission and he went west with the band.

They started up the Hayes River, crossed into the Nelson and then into the Saskatchewan. At The Pas they found two French Canadian traders who threatened to keep Henday a prisoner. But Big Elk just laughed again and said, "They dare not keep you," and they did not dare.

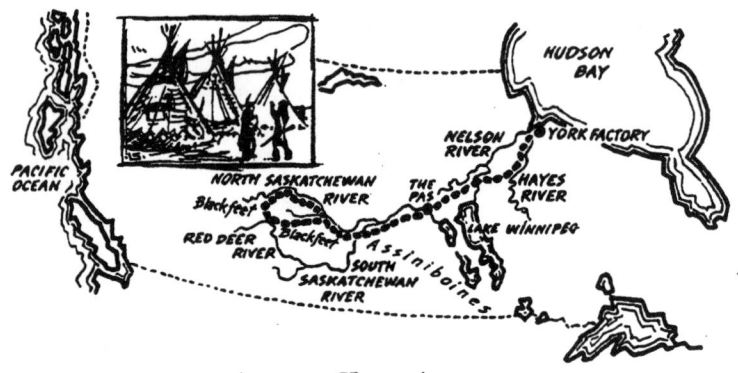

ANTHONY HENDAY'S ROUTE

In August, the Assiniboines reached their hunting ground on the Red Deer River. They held a feast of thanksgiving for their safe return, and then the young men went buffalo hunting. Henday says that the buffalo were so thick there that they found it hard to keep out of their way. The young men were good buffalo hunters, but, on another hunt, two of them were wounded by grizzly bears and one died.

In October, the Assiniboines moved to the South Saskatchewan River where they met the Blackfeet. Henday was astonished to see them on horseback. Long before this the Spaniards had brought horses to Mexico. Some of them had escaped and become wild. These wild horses slowly moved north. All across the western plains some of them were captured and broken in; now all the far western tribes rode horses.

The chiefs of the Blackfeet held a council and Henday was invited to it. After the peace pipes had been smoked, the Chief of the Assiniboines told the Blackfeet that Henday had been sent by the Great Chief who lived by the Great Water to invite their young men to take their furs to him. But the Chief of the Blackfeet shook his head.

"It is too far off," he said. "My young men ride like the wind. They cannot sit paddling in canoes; that is for the prairie tribes. Tell your Chief that my people cannot come."

Henday spent that winter hunting with his band on the North Saskatchewan and, in the spring, they went down to the Bay with sixty canoes loaded with furs.

## 2. Peter Pond led the Canadians into Athabaska.

By this time several Canadian fur trading teams were trading around Lake Winnipeg. At first they traded against one another. Each team tried to offer more goods for a skin than the other teams. They soon saw that that did not pay and Alexander Henry suggested that he, Peter Pond, and the Frobisher brothers should be partners. They united and made up a party of thirty canoes and one hundred and thirty men to go up to The Pas.

There they were met by Chief Chatique, a huge fierce-looking Indian with a band of thirty painted warriors as big as himself. Chatique invited the traders into his tent. The Canadians were afraid, but they dared

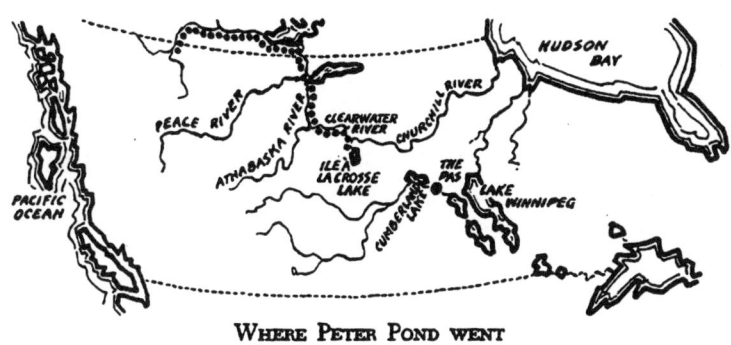

WHERE PETER POND WENT

**TRADERS**

not refuse. The Chief welcomed them politely and then told them that he could easily kill them, but that he would not do so if they gave him rich presents. They gave him rich presents.

They were glad to get away from there and paddled on up the river as fast as they could. At Cumberland Lake, they found a new Hudson's Bay trading post that had been built the year before. While the French Canadian traders had been away fighting for Canada, the Western tribes had been taking their furs down to the Hudson's Bay Company. Now the partners planned that the Frobishers would cross over to the Churchill River and meet the Indians on their way down to the Bay. They found them on Ile a la Crosse Lake and got a great stock of furs.

The Canadians did so well that time that they planned to build other posts west and north of Cumberland House to meet the Indians on their way to the Bay. They sent Peter Pond to build a post in Athabaska. Pond's native guides led him to Ile a la Crosse Lake; then they portaged over a high ridge of land into the Clearwater River. Paddling west, they came to the Athabaska River where Pond built Fort Athabaska.

There the Canadians got the furs of all the Indians of the north and far west. Fort Athabaska was a very rich post; it faced west across the wide, beautiful valley of the Peace River to the Rocky Mountains and the Pacific Ocean. From the Fort to the Pacific was the last lap of the great Canadian relay race. In the long summer after his furs had been sent down to Montreal, Peter talked with the Indians about the rivers leading to the mountains, drew maps, and dreamed of winning the relay race. But Peter was not to be the winner. He had been in trouble. A man was killed and Pond was blamed for it. The new North West Company of Montreal sent Alexander Mackenzie to take over Fort Athabaska and to find the way to the Pacific.

Peter must have felt sad, but he did not blame anyone. He told Mackenzie all that the Indians had told him about the rivers, showed him his maps and, in the spring, went down with the fur brigade to his home in the east. The fur brigade was the long line of canoes which, every Spring, took the furs to Montreal and brought back supplies for the men.

### 3. Alexander Mackenzie won the great relay race.

Alexander Mackenzie was a young Scotsman who had begun to work for the North West Company when he was sixteen. He had done well and was now a member of the Company. He brought his cousin, Roderick Mackenzie, up to take charge of the trading post while he was away. Roderick was a good trader; everyone liked him. He moved the trading post down the river to Lake Athabaska and named it Fort Chipewyan. He soon made Chipewyan the busiest post in the west. He even had time to start the first library in the north-west.

During the winter Alexander made his plans and got everything ready. Then, in June, as soon as Roderick had gone down to Montreal with the furs, Alexander started for the Pacific. He and his friends headed west, but they got into the Mackenzie River which soon turned north. They went on, hoping it would turn west again, but it never did. On July 11, Mackenzie climbed a hill and saw the Arctic ice-pack stretching right round from west to east. He saw Inuit houses too, and whales spouting. Mackenzie knew then that he had reached not the Pacific, but the Arctic Ocean. It was a great disappointment, but Mackenzie did not give up. He paddled back (upstream this time) to Fort Chipewyan and began to prepare to explore the Peace River. Perhaps that would lead him to the Pacific.

In two years he was ready. This time he and his men just paddled round the bend from the Fort into the Peace River and kept straight on. The river kept on westward for a long time, running through beautiful country so full of beaver, deer, and buffalo that it looked like a great pasture field. But this time the voyageurs were moving upstream, and the river often ran so swiftly that they could not paddle against it. They had to land, climb the bank, and track or drag the canoe through the water with a long

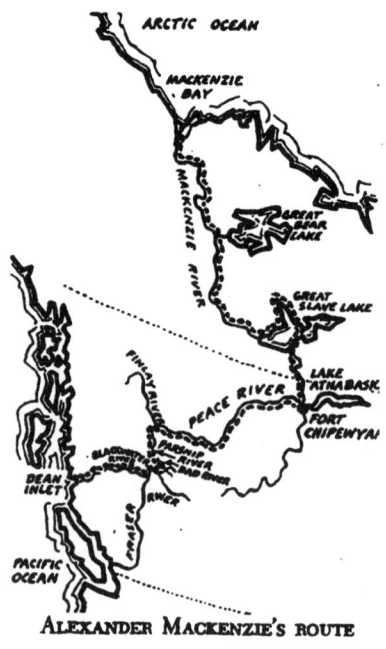

ALEXANDER MACKENZIE'S ROUTE

rope.

They were excited when they first saw the Rocky Mountains with the sun shining on their snowy peaks. They got into them through the Peace River Canyon, a twenty-mile-long stretch of rapids and falls between high walls of rock. The rapids flung the canoe from one wall to the other. The men could not even track her. They had to land, haul her up the canyon wall and carry her through the woods to a quieter stretch of river.

Next they came to the place where the Parsnip and Finlay Rivers meet to form the Peace. They could not tell which to take, but an old Indian told them to take the Parsnip. They did so, but by mistake got into the Bad River where they had to wade and drag the canoe most of the time. The men were nearly worn out, but Mackenzie gave them extra rations and cheered them on, and presently they got into the Fraser. They were now among Indians who had big villages and lived on salmon. These Indians were warlike and were hostile to the voyageurs, but Mackenzie managed to make peace with them. The Indians told him he could not get down the Fraser, but should take a path that ran by the Blackwater River to the coast.

That cheered them all. They cached their canoe and tramped away down the path. Some of the Indians they met were friendly, others were not, but they marched on, feasting on salmon and expecting any day to come out upon the shore of the Pacific. They reached it at Dean Inlet. Mackenzie mixed red colour with oil and painted his name and the date on a great rock there. He and his men were the first to cross Canada from the Atlantic to the Pacific. They had won the great relay race.

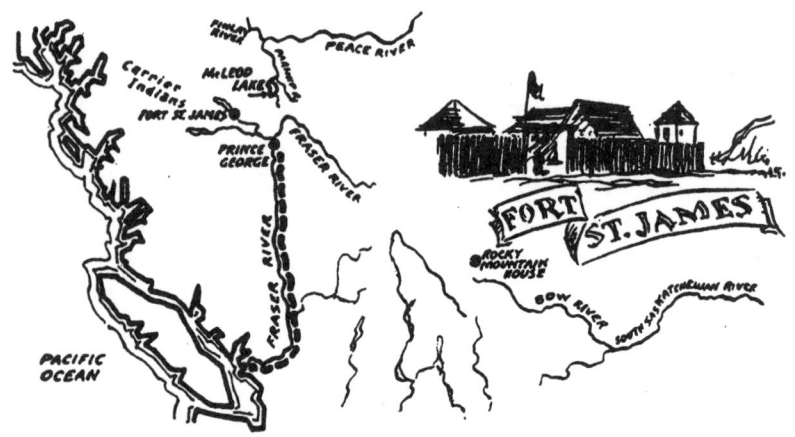

SIMON FRASER BUILT FORT ST. JAMES

## 4. Simon Fraser won the race for the Fraser River country.

Each year now the North West Company was building trading posts farther and farther west. The Hudson's Bay Company was building posts, too, but had not yet caught up with the Nor' Westers. After Alexander Mackenzie had found a way through the Rocky Mountains to the Pacific, the North West Company sent Simon Fraser to build trading posts west of the mountains.

Fraser worked quickly. He built Rocky Mountain House, and sent James McDougall forward to build on McLeod Lake. While McDougall did that, Fraser went on west and built Fort St. James among the Carrier Indians. They were glad to have a trading post in their country. The Carriers lived on salmon and, as the salmon were late coming up the rivers that year, the Carriers had only berries to eat and almost starved till the salmon came. Then the Indians feasted, and afterwards dried great piles of the fish for the winter.

By that time the American traders were in California and the Russians in Alaska, but the space between had not been taken up. Mackenzie had taken possession of it for Canada, but the Canadians had no settlements there. To hold it they must build trading posts there. Everybody thought that Fraser's river was the Columbia, and that the Americans were making for it, so the Nor'Westers ordered Fraser to take it for Canada and to be quick about it.

Fraser had already built Fort George as a starting point, so he set off at once. The Indians had told Mackenzie that he would not be able to take canoes down this wild river. Fraser and his men did it, but they had a terrible trip. The canoes raced through canyon after canyon, thrown wildly from wall to wall, ripped and torn by the rocks. The men risked their lives every day running the terrible rapids. At last a few brave men agreed to take the canoes on, while the others landed and went forward on horseback.

By this time Fraser knew that his river was not the Columbia; it was too far north for that. It was a new river that no one had known about. Fraser did not quite reach the sea; the coast Indians were so threatening that, to save his men, he just quickly claimed the country for Canada and went home.

**5. David Thompson lost the race for the Columbia.**

Like Henry Kelsey, David Thompson was a poor boy in London. Kind people got him into a school where he became very good at arithmetic. When he was fourteen, the Hudson's Bay Company chose him to go to Canada. He spent the first winter at Cumberland House where he was fascinated by the glittering winter stars and sat up for thirty-five nights studying them. He taught himself to measure distances by them and became a famous geographer and map-maker. After eight years, he left the Old Company and

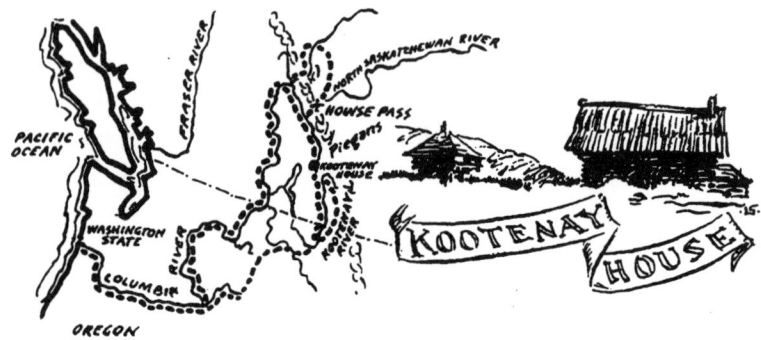
DAVID THOMPSON'S ROUTE

joined the Nor'Westers. For them he traded, and also surveyed (mapped) much of western Canada.

Thompson was a patient and careful explorer. It wasn't enough for him to find the shortest route from one trading post to the next; he took his time to study the plants and animals, to get to know the natives, and to write everything down so that other people could read about his discoveries. When we read his journals we can learn a lot about life in North America two hundred years ago.

The North West Company now wanted to build a trading post at the mouth of the Columbia River. The traders wanted to bring their goods in, and take their furs out, by ship. Carrying goods by ship is much cheaper than hauling them over land. The Company also wanted to take as much of the Pacific coast for Canada as they could. Before Fraser went down his river, Thompson had escaped the Piegan Indians, who tried to stop him - that is a good story - and got through the Howse Pass in the Rocky Mountains at the upper part of the Columbia River. He did not know for sure that it was the Columbia, but he thought it was. Thompson built a trading post there, and another on the Kootenay River where he and his men had many exciting encounters with the natives.

After Fraser had found that his river was not the Columbia, the Nor'Westers kept begging Thompson to go down to the mouth of his river to make sure that it was the Columbia, to take possession of the land there for Canada, and to build a trading post. But Thompson did not hurry; he took his time building posts and trading, and carefully surveying the upper part of his river. Suddenly the Nor'Westers heard that an American ship was coming to take the mouth of the Columbia. Then Thompson tried to hurry. But he waited for more men, and stopped to build a new cedar canoe. When he reached the sea he found the Americans there with their post partly built.

So the Americans got the mouth of the Columbia and began to trade for furs there. But Thompson had mapped much of the interior of that land which is now the states of Washington and Oregon. Canadian fur traders continued to do business there for many years. Many years later Britain and the United States made an agreement giving the territory to the Americans. Thompson, who was by then an old man, was bitterly disappointed.

We can be proud of David Thompson who is considered the greatest map-maker who ever lived.

# 14    Red River Was the First Settlement in Western Canada

**1811 to 1866**

**1. The Silver Chief started the Red River settlement.**

There had been another big war in Europe and many British men fought in it. When it was over and the men came home, they could not find jobs. They wandered around starving and begging.

Lord Selkirk (the Silver Chief) was a Scottish earl. He was rich, kind, and a member of the Hudson's Bay Company. He was so sorry for the homeless Scots that he bought a large block of land on the Red River from the Hudson's Bay Company, and sent 105 poor men out to begin farming in the New World. It was fall when they got to York Factory, so they had to spend the winter there.

It took them all the next summer to get their goods up to their land at Fort Rouge (Winnipeg), Verendrye's old trading post, on the Red River. It was now the North West Company's Fort Gibraltar. The traders did not want settlers there, but when the tired farmers arrived, the Nor'Westers helped them set up their tents and sold them grain and potatoes. As it was too late to begin farming, their Governor, Macdonell, moved the settlers up to Pembina where the Nor'Westers let them join the Company's buffalo hunt. After that they had enough food for the winter.

In the spring they hurried back to their farms. They had only hoes to work with, but they scratched up small plots. The soil was so rich that the wheat came up thick and tall. They were very proud of it, but till it was ripe they had to live on berries and fish, and fight from dawn to dark to keep huge flocks of birds off their crops. More settlers came each year, and soon Red River was on its feet.

**2. The Nor'Westers tried to destroy Red River.**

The Nor'Westers had been kind to the first settlers because they did not think they would stay. The fur traders had always said that nothing would grow on the prairies. When they saw the Selkirk settlers' good crops they were afraid that people would rush in and drive away the fur-bearing animals. The Company sent in Duncan Cameron, a jolly Scot, who persuaded most of the settlers to move to Ontario where they were given good farms.

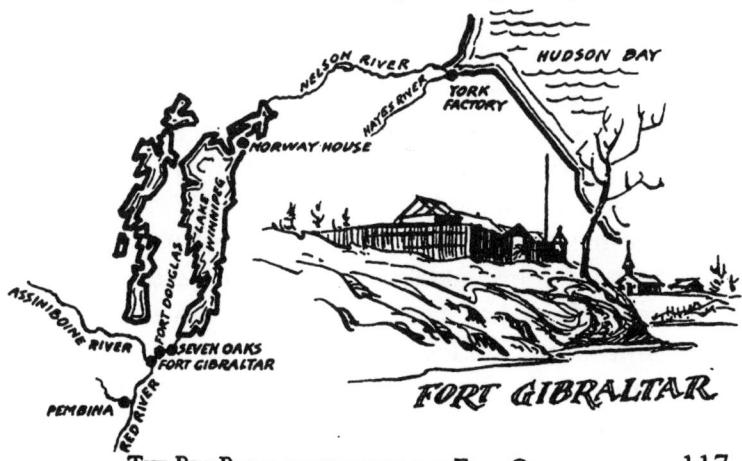

THE RED RIVER SETTLEMENT AND FORT GIBRALTAR

But quite a few families remained loyal to Lord Selkirk and refused to go. When the Nor'Westers of Fort Gibraltar attacked them, the families fled to Lake Winnipeg, but a party of men gathered in John McLeod's blacksmith's shop to defend themselves. To prevent a fight, Governor Macdonell gave himself up, and the Nor'Westers carried him a prisoner to Fort William.

But Scots do not give in easily. When Lord Selkirk heard Macdonell's story, he sent Colin Robertson to bring his settlers back to their homes and sent Robert Semple, a new Governor, with a hundred new settlers to start more farms. Semple and Robertson were soldiers. They captured the Nor'Westers' Fort Gibraltar, strengthened their own Fort Douglas, and felt safe.

The Nor'Westers then decided to get the Metis involved. In the early days there were no white women in the west, so the fur traders married Indian women. Their children were part Indian and part white and were called Metis (mixed). Many of the Metis girls were very pretty and made good wives, and the young men were good hunters and voyageurs. Their fathers were proud of them, and some fathers sent their sons to England to be educated.

The Metis felt that the west was their country, and they were afraid that the settlers would take it from them. In the spring Cuthbert Grant, the Metis leader, with a large band swept down upon the settlement. Governor Semple and his men met them at Seven Oaks. While the leaders talked, Semple laid his hand on one of the Metis' guns. He meant no harm, but a Metis fired at him and a fight began. Semple and twenty of his men were killed.

Lord Selkirk had been begging the Government to give him some soldiers to protect his people. The Government refused, so he hired a band of Swiss soldiers,

A MÉTIS FAMILY

raced them up to the Lakes, recaptured Fort Douglas, and settled his people on their farms again. He had their farms surveyed, planned for a church and a school, roads and a mill. He called a Council of the Indian chiefs, smoked the peace pipe, and made a treaty with them. He won their hearts by his friendliness. It was they who named him "the Silver Chief".

But the North West Company said that what Lord Selkirk had done was against the law. He was arrested and tried, but before he was sentenced he became ill and died. His Red River settlement has grown into the great city of Winnipeg, the capital of the province of Manitoba.

**3. The two companies united as the Hudson's Bay Company.**

The North West Company and the Hudson's Bay Company had always been rivals for the fur trade of the west. Each one tried to get as many furs as it could. At first there were plenty of furs for both companies, and they were friendly rivals. They took in each other's lost men, lent each other canoes, or food, and sometimes built their posts inside the same palisade for company.

But as more and more men hunted them, the animals became fewer, and the companies became unfriendly rivals. Each tried to do the other as much harm as possible. The Hudson's Bay Company had the Bay, which was the shortest and cheapest way to ship the furs to England, and refused to let the North West Company use it. The North West Company had Athabaska, the best fur country, and fought to keep the Hudson's Bay traders out of it.

So it went on, the war growing fiercer every year. The Nor' Westers had the best of it, for all their traders were partners in the company and fought furiously, while the Hudson's Bay men were on salary and did not fight back so hard. But they did fight and the war was ruining both companies. The heads of the companies saw this, so they held meetings and after long discussions the two companies united as the Hudson's Bay Company.

### 4. Governor George Simpson was young and merry.

The union succeeded. And that is the story of George Simpson, the first governor of the united Company. It is a jolly, fast-moving story, for Simpson was a jolly, fast-

Norway House

moving young man. He had his office at Norway House on Lake Winnipeg, but he spent most of his time racing back and forth across the continent in his big red canoe, paddled by eight Iroquois voyageurs. There is a story that once, when Simpson was shouting at them to paddle faster, one of the big Iroquois picked up little George by the back of his coat and dipped him in the lake.

Simpson was a strict inspector. He crossed the country every year, stopping at all the posts, questioning them about their business, going through their account books, and giving them their orders. But he was also young and fun-loving and he enjoyed parties and dancing. So whenever word came to a post that the Governor was coming, the traders there invited in all the traders and natives in the district, and there was a grand dinner and dance.

Simpson loved to travel. In spite of his many journeys to the trading posts, he never seemed to tire of it. He once invited a few friends to cross the continent with him. They took two canoes well filled with food, each paddled by nine famous voyageurs. They left York Factory with the big guns firing and people cheering, and paddled west

GOVERNOR GEORGE SIMPSON

to Norway House. By the time they got there, they were looking a little untidy, so they landed three miles off, washed, shaved, and put on their best clothes. Then, with paddles flashing, bagpipes and bugles playing, they dashed up to the wharf where the trader and his family and all the Indians for miles around were gathered. Then for two days Simpson inspected books and men all day, and everybody danced most of the night.

News that they were coming was always far ahead of them. Every post was ready to be inspected and to give them a good time. They finished their journey at Fort Langley near the mouth of the Fraser River. They had crossed North America at its widest part, by canoe, in ninety days.

## 5. Enter British Columbia

For several years Governor Simpson dashed round the west building up the fur trade. When he had put the prairie trading posts in order, he went on to British Columbia. Trader James Douglas was doing well at Fort St. James, but sending furs 1200 miles across to Hudson Bay was expensive. Dr. McLoughlin at Fort Vancouver used ships to send his furs to England

and to get his supplies, and this was much cheaper.

"We must bring the northern furs down to Fort Vancouver," said Simpson. The Company did that by opening the Okanagan Trail. The traders now took the northern furs on pack horses down to Fort Kamloops, rested and changed horses there, and then took them on to the Okanagan where boats waited to take them to Fort Vancouver and the ships. The men brought the supplies north in the same way, and the Company saved money.

They started a horse ranch at Kamloops where the pack trains changed horses. John Tod was the trader there. He was a big, jolly man, a friend of Lolo, Chief of the Shuswaps. The story is that once when Tod's men went down to the Fraser to catch salmon, the Shuswaps waited by the river to kill them. Lolo told Tod of the plan, and Tod rode forward alone to face the Indians. He threw down his sword and pistol in front of them and asked what they wanted.

"Lolo!" they said. "Where is he?"

"He is at home," said Tod. "Haven't you heard that the smallpox is upon us? But I have come to save you. Let each wash his right arm in the river and then come to me."

All Indians were terrified of the smallpox and they did as he told them. They lined up and he vaccinated them. He gave a good deep cut to their right arms so that they would not be able to use them for a while. That ended the Shuswaps' conspiracy.

# 15

## The Pioneers
### 1815 to 1850

**1. Next came the pioneers; they worked hard.**

Britain and France had been fighting a war. When it was over and the British men came home, there was not enough land or work for them in Britain. But in Canada there were big stretches of land waiting to be farmed, so the workless people began to stream over. Those who had no money to pay the passage on the ships borrowed from their friends. Many towns paid the passage money for their homeless people. Land companies bought large blocks of land in Canada and took over people who promised to pay for their land when they had sold their crops.

Most of the pioneers had large families and they all worked hard. On the farm everyone got up at four o'clock in the morning. In the Stewart family, Andrew, the oldest boy, raked the ashes off the coals in the fire-place and puffed at them with the bellows till they blazed up. Sometimes all his puffing did not make a blaze. The fire was out. Then he had to waken young Charlie and send him running to the neighbours to borrow a live coal. Charlie ran back with it glowing between two chips and soon had a fire going. "Chips" are dried cow manure which makes good kindling. Charlie then whistled to Rover and raced off to fetch the cows.

A PIONEER KITCHEN

Meantime Father Stewart and the big boys were busy in the barn, feeding the animals and doing other chores. Hannah and Jessie were getting breakfast. Betsy made the beds while Mother Stewart with Isabel and young Johnny went up to the barn to help Charlie with the milking. Except when there was snow on the ground, the children all went barefoot and, on frosty mornings, they hopped from chip to chip across the yard.

When the men and the milkers returned, Mother strained the milk into pans. The men took turns at the wash-basin, and they sat down to breakfast, except Isabel and Johnny. The youngest children stood at the table to eat in those days. They all bowed their heads and Father said a long blessing. Then Mother poured the tea and the girls filled the bowls with porridge and milk. Isabel and Johnny had only one bowl between them. They drew a line through the middle of their porridge with their spoons, and dared not quarrel for they stood next to Father. Then Jessie dished up the ham. The big plates of bread and bowls of apple sauce went round. Sometimes Mother and Father had butter on their bread.

When breakfast was over, the men went to work in the fields. Harvest was over; they had cut their grain with a scythe and threshed it with a flail. Now they were digging potatoes. The children ran off to school, Isabel carrying their ham sandwiches in a cotton bag. They walked two miles to school, and met other children on the way. It was fun.

At home, Hannah baked bread, johnny-cake, gingerbread, pans of biscuits and cookies, a dozen pies. She said that food just melted in that family. Jessie did the housework, and Betsy sat down at her spinning-wheel, for she made the family's clothes. She spun the wool into yarn, wove the yarn into cloth, cut out and sewed the clothes by hand. She had to work all day, nearly every day, to keep the family dressed.

Meantime Mother Stewart doctored her sick calf, fed her chickens and got out her dye tub, for Betsy had twenty skeins of yarn spun and ready to be dyed. Then she started the fire under her soap kettle, and damped down the coal in the smoke house where the ham was being smoked. By that time the girls had dinner ready and Betsy blew the horn that hung outside the kitchen door to call the men to meals.

**2. The pioneers had fun too.**

The girls hurried dinner that day for they were going to a party in the evening. The Robsons were having an apple-paring bee. A bee is a jolly kind of party. At a bee the neighbours gather at one home to help the owner to do a certain kind of work. The pioneers had many kinds of bees: house-building, ploughing, threshing, quilting, apple-paring. You can have a bee to do almost any kind of work.

AN APPLE-PARING BEE

There were twenty-two young men and girls at the Robson's bee that night. The apples were ripe, and Mrs. Robson wanted to dry some sacks of them for the winter. The guests found the two kitchen tables laid with knives and bowls, and they drew up benches beside them. The girls took their places and a boy sat between each two girls.

The young men peeled the apples; the girls cored and sliced them till they had a bowlful. The bowls were then passed to the children who sat by the fire-place stringing the thick slices with darning needles on strong threads. The Robson girls hung the strings on racks to dry. The dried apples were sweet and chewy. Pioneer children snatched handfuls of them whenever they could to eat as candy.

With so many hands at work the apples were soon pared. Mrs. Robson had the tea ready. The girls set out plates piled high with sandwiches, cake, cookies, pears, and maple sugar. Everyone had a good supper. Then they pushed back the tables. The fiddler set his chair on one of them and began to play. The dance began; most bees ended in a dance.

### 3. The pioneers were great builders.

The pioneers had to be road builders. The Loyalists had settled along the shores of the lakes and rivers, and had used boats for transportation. The pioneers had to take farms behind the Loyalists, so they had to pick their way through the woods on foot, or on horseback, to reach their land.

The first roads were just narrow paths winding round the stumps, rocks, and mudholes. The wagons bumped so much that people were often thrown out and sometimes killed. So the pioneers tried to make better roads by taking out the stumps and laying logs close together side by side. These roads were called corduroy roads, for they were ridged like corrugated paper. Though the wagons still bumped, the bumps were small bouncy ones. Then someone thought of covering the logs with a good thick layer of dirt. The dirt roads were dusty, but smoother than those made of logs.

Stage coaches now ran on all the main roads. They were like our buses, but smaller, and without springs. They had seats inside and outside. Boys liked to sit outside with the coachman. Sometimes he let them drive his four-horse team. That was very exciting, especially when they galloped into a town with the conductor blowing his horn to warn the people. The stage coaches had to stop about every twenty miles or so to change horses and give the passengers time to get a bite to eat.

Winter was the pleasantest time to travel in pioneer days, for then everyone went in sleighs. The pioneers filled the bottom of the sleigh with straw, put on all their warm clothes, and wrapped buffalo robes round themselves. Then they raced away, smoothly and swiftly, with sleigh bells making music all the way. Sleigh bells

SLEIGHING

made the merriest music and sleighing parties were the greatest fun! The boys and girls drove round for a while, laughing and singing. Then perhaps the driver tipped them all out in the snow. How they yelled! Then he drove them to the house of a friend who had a hot supper ready for them.

By this time, steamboats had been invented. The first one was called the *Accommodation*. She ran the 170 miles from Montreal to Quebec in a day and a half, instead of in four or five days as the sailing ships did. At first many people thought it was wicked to travel so fast; others were afraid to go on her for fear she would blow up. But they soon got over that, and before long, steamships were running on all our lakes and rivers.

Next they had to build a canal to let the steamboats pass through the Lachine Rapids into Lake Ontario. That canal worked so well that they decided to build one round Niagara Falls to let the boats up into Lake Erie. The Falls are 160 feet high. The canal had to be twenty-four miles long; it took a long time to build and cost a lot of money, but they did it. After that, canals between the lakes were easy. Soon Canadians could sail all the way from the Atlantic Ocean to Lake Superior.

AN EARLY TRAIN

The next excitement? Can you guess? Yes, a railway. By this time railways were being built in England, and Canada wasn't going to be left behind. Our first railway ran from the St. Lawrence opposite Montreal to the Richelieu River. It was sixteen miles long, and it had wooden rails with flat strips of iron nailed on top. It had four cars. For the first year they were hauled along the rails by horses, but the next year an engine was used, so small that they called her the "Kitten". The Governor and a large crowd of people came down to see her start. When the great moment came and the crowd stood breathless, "Kitten" *wouldn't* start!

"Give her more wood and water," shouted the engineer. They did, and the "Kitten" dashed away with her cars rattling behind her at twenty miles an hour. How the people cheered! They had never seen anything go as fast as that in their lives.

**4. Canada got two new kinds of business.**

Canada's first business was fur trading. She made much money out of that. Her next business was farming. The French Canadians began both of these trades. The

Loyalists and most of the pioneers were farmers. But in Britain's war with Napoleon Canada got a third business: she became a big timber merchant.

When the first settlers cleared their land, they chopped down the trees and burned them. No one wanted to buy timber then. But when England was fighting her war with Napoleon, she needed a great deal of big timber to build ships for her navy. In those days eastern Canada was covered with beautiful woods, so Britain began to buy timber from her. Canada went into the timber and lumber business.

The timber companies paid high wages and thousands of young Canadians went into the woods. They lived in camps and wore bright clothes and big boots. When they had cut down the trees, they hauled them to the river where men tied them together into rafts to float them down the rivers to Quebec, or to Saint John. The rafts had to be very strong to float through the many rapids without being broken into pieces.

The "River Drivers" rode the rafts down. They set up tents, or built shacks on them. Sometimes they took their families with them. Running the rapids must have been great fun for the children; but frightening, too, for sometimes the rafts were smashed and the people drowned. At the wildest rapids they built timber slides of boards and ran the rafts down them. That was like sleigh-riding down a steep hill. In Quebec and Saint John, the rafts were broken up and loaded onto the English ships waiting for them. Our Canadian timber helped Britain to win the war against Napoleon.

Canada's fourth big business was ship-building. Quebec and Ontario built ships, too, but it was the Maritime provinces that made Canada world famous for her ship-building. There, captains often built their ships

SHIP-BUILDING

with their own hands. They used big timbers for the keel, tough spruce for the ribs, plenty of planks to board her in, and tall pines for the masts. The builder had only to choose a good bit of shore to build on, get his men and go to work. How proud they were when their ship was finished! Then, shining with white paint, she shook out her white sails and sailed out of the harbour to begin carrying goods and people all over the world.

The seaside provinces had the men to sail their ships, too. Boys often went to sea when they were ten years old. Teen-agers did men's work, and were such good sailors that many of them became officers before they were twenty. There are hundreds of good stories of their adventures. Their ships sailed so fast that they were called "clippers". Merchants who had valuable cargoes like silk or tea always shipped them in the tall, white clippers if they could. For a long time they were the queens of the sea.

At last Quebec offered $15,000 to anyone who would build a fast steamboat to run between Quebec and Halifax. A Halifax company took the work. James Goudie planned her and George Black built her. She was the biggest steamship in Canada, with cabins and an elegant parlour for the passengers. There was a grand party at her launching. She was named the *Royal William*. She made the return trip to Halifax in five days, not counting stops at ports. Sailing ships took from two to three weeks. The Halifax people were amazed to see her arrive so soon. Two years later she became the first steamship to cross the Atlantic.

# 16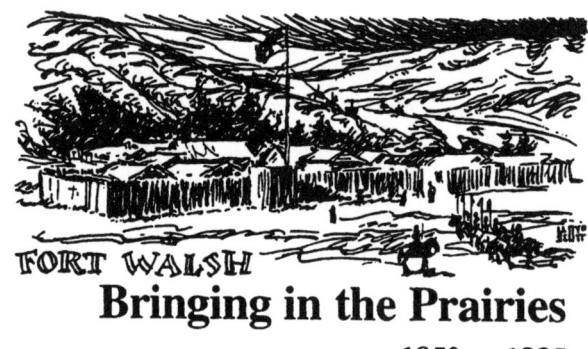
## Bringing in the Prairies
### 1850 to 1885

**1. The people of the great plains**

THE INDIANS HUNT THE BUFFALO. In pioneer days the buffalo roamed across the prairies in thousands. The Indians' summer hunt began in June. The evening before the start, the band elected a chief of the hunt, ten captains, and ten or more scouts. Then they made the "laws of the hunt". The main law was that no one should chase buffalo before the chief gave the word. Anyone who did so was to have his saddle and bridle cut up.

Next morning, the squaws took down the tents, loaded everything onto the carts, and the band started for the herd. When the scouts signalled "buffalo seen", all was excitement. The women made camp. The hunters mounted, strapped their powder horns to their belts, took their bullets in their mouths and waited, the horses dancing, as excited as the men.

The chief gives the word, the horses leap ahead and race for the hill from which the scouts signal. They look down from it across a plain ten miles wide by twenty

WAITING FOR THE SIGNAL

miles long, black with buffalo. Gun in hand and every eye on the chief they wait for the signal. He gives it. Now! Guiding their horses with their knees, swift as an arrow's flight, they hurl themselves at the herd.

When the hunt was over, the hunters cut up the dead buffalo and the squaws loaded the meat onto the carts to carry it to the camp. There they cut it into strips and hung it on poles to dry in the sun. Three days in the sun dried it enough to fold into bundles. When the Indians wanted to eat it, the dried meat was placed in a wooden bowl and pounded to powder. Mixed with berries and hot grease and then cooled, it made pemmican, a very nourishing food.

THE BAD MEN. The Hudson's Bay Company had always feared the fierce Blackfoot and Blood tribes of the south-west, and had kept out of their country. But in the United States settlers were moving north-west. Many of those who came first were outlaws, bad men pushed out by the decent people. These bad men began riding across the boundary into Canada and selling liquor to our Indians. It maddened them. They robbed their families and killed each other for it. Then the whiskey traders built Fort Whoop-Up in Canada. They built it with strong doors that shut off their living-rooms from the trading rooms, so that the crazed Indians could not break in on them.

Next, a group of smugglers chased by the American police fled across the boundary into Canada where their officers could not follow them. They, too, built a strong fort and began whiskey trading. Soon there were several whiskey trading posts in the south-west, and all along the boundary line evil men were driving wagon loads of whiskey across into Canada. Not only the Indians, but white settlers, too, were drinking and killing one another.

**2. Canada sent the North West Mounted Police to keep order.**

When Canada heard of these wild doings, the Government sent men to stop them. The Americans had sent an army against their Indians and had fought a long war with them. Canada wanted to put her west in order by law instead of by fighting, so she sent policemen. The Government chose three hundred young men, strong, educated, and able to ride. They were trained as mounted policemen. They were the first of Canada's famous "Mounted Police", but they travelled west by train. Our railway was not yet built, so they had to go through the United States.

The proud young "Mounties" wore scarlet coats, grey breeches, white helmets with plumes, and jack-boots. Each man carried a rifle and a revolver, and the officers wore swords. They left the train at Fargo in the United States, and marched north to Dufferin, Manitoba. There they turned west along the Boundary Road with a long train of carts, wagons, cattle for meat, cows for milk, mowing machines, and other implements, all strung out behind them. They needed these things because they were marching through empty country, and they planned to build police posts in it.

Day after day they marched from morning till night across dry plains where there was little food for the animals, and little water even for the men. When they reached a river they had to wade through it. Always they kept watch for bad white men and painted Indian warriors. For weeks they met no one. Then, in the Cypress Hills, Indians began to slip into their camp. They told the police that the whiskey traders were hiding, but that they would come back when the police had gone. The traders did not know that the police had come to stay.

Sure enough, when the Police Force reached the Bow River, not a whiskey trader could they find. Colonel Macleod led his troops against Fort Whoop-Up; he and his men stopped on the hill above it. The big gates were closed. Nothing moved. With guns ready the police rode

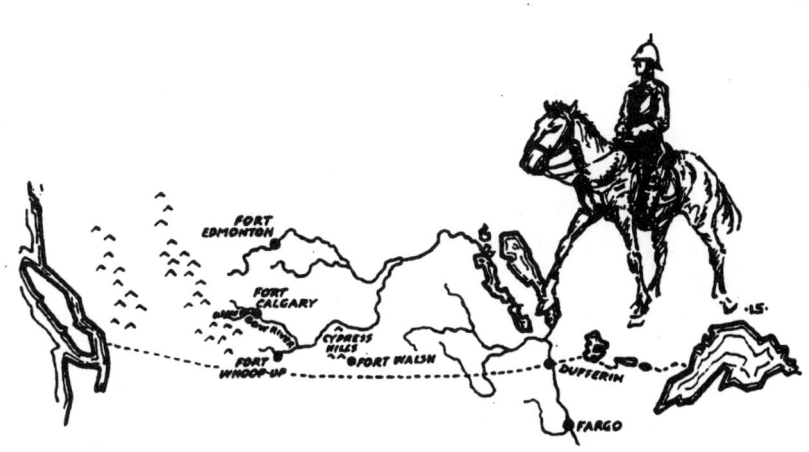

THE NORTH WEST MOUNTED POLICE WERE SENT WEST

down the hill and pounded on the gate. No one answered. At last they heard a step. The gate opened a crack and an old Indian peeped out. He gave a terrified yell and fled. The police dismounted and went in. A lame caretaker met them. He said that the whiskey men were away trading, but that the Police were welcome to come in. They went in; Fort Whoop-Up was captured. How their comrades teased them about that great victory!

Their leader, Commissioner French, then sent Inspector Walsh to build a post at Edmonton. Later, Fort Walsh was built in the Cypress Hills, and Fort Calgary at the meeting of the Bow and Elbow Rivers.

PRAIRIE CHICKEN OLD MAN. Colonel Macleod, the commander in the south-west, had Jerry Potts, a clever Metis, as his guide. Jerry brought him word that Prairie Chicken Old Man had been killing cattle and was hiding in Chief Red Crow's camp. Colonel Macleod sent two policemen to arrest him. They rode into the camp and seized him, but the braves and squaws tore him from the Police. Macleod then sent twenty men with Jerry Potts to fetch him. The Police halted outside and Jerry went into the camp. Red Crow was smoking his pipe. " T h e Police have come for Prairie Chicken Old Man," said Jerry.

"Tell them I will think about it," said Red Crow.

"The Inspector says that if you don't bring him out in an hour, the Police will ride in and take both of you," said Jerry.

Red Crow smoked on, but the band made a great uproar.

A mile away the Police waited on their horses. The Inspector held his watch open in his hand. No one came from the camp. The minutes passed. The Inspector

CHIEF SITTING BULL

snapped his watch shut. The Police straightened up ready to ride, when over the rise came the Indians with Red Crow. The Police marched them all into Fort Macleod where Colonel Macleod scolded them well and sent Prairie Chicken Old Man to prison for a while. Red Crow and his band watched what was done without a word, and then went home quietly. They had learned how the white policemen kept law and order.

THE SITTING BULL STORY. The Americans had been fighting with their Indians for a long time. Sitting Bull, the great Chief of the Sioux, set a trap for General Custer and his regiment. The regiment fell into the trap and the Sioux killed nearly all of them. The Government of the United States then sent a big army to punish Sitting Bull, but he and his tribe fled over the boundary into Canada. They pitched their camp near Fort Walsh and settled down. They knew that they were safe in Canada.

The Mounted Police had plenty of work keeping their own Indians in order and they tried to get the Sioux to go home, but they would not go. The Americans promised that they would not punish them, and that they would give them new lands and cattle. The Sioux would not budge. They made plenty of trouble for the Police. Once the

Sioux killed and scalped six of our Indians. The Police put the murderers in prison. Sitting Bull hurled himself angrily upon Sergeant MacDonald, but the policeman took him quietly by the arm into his office and explained the law to him. Sitting Bull gave in and the murderers were tried and hanged. The Sioux stayed four years in Canada, but at last the Mounted Police persuaded them to go home.

### 3. The Canadians built the Canadian Pacific Railway to tie the provinces together.

Canada had already built a railway to connect Quebec and Ontario with the Maritime provinces. The Prime Minister Sir John Macdonald, had promised British Columbia one, too, and the Government began to build it. At first the railway did not get on very fast, but after Sir William Van Horne was made manager it grew like magic.

The part through the rough land north of Lakes Huron and Superior was very hard to build. But Van Horne did not wait to finish that. He kept his eye on that part and at the same time set the men building from Winnipeg west across the prairies. That was an easy piece to build, but all the timber and steel and food for the men had to be brought from eastern Canada. Still Van Horne kept the men racing west.

They built hundreds of camps across the hundreds of miles of prairie, and hundreds of horses and mules drew hundreds of wagons of food, ties, and steel rails from camp to camp. Thousands of men worked from dawn till dark, each gang trying to beat the next one. The surveyors marked out the line of the railway. The graders shovelled up the "grade" and flattened it. The track-layers followed their leader, seven-foot-tall Donald Gordon, laying down the ties and spiking the rails to them. Soon Van Horne and Donald had them laying three and a half miles of track a day and, in a grand burst of speed they once laid twenty miles in three days.

It was hard work building through the mountains. Even Big Donald could not lay rails quickly there. The men had to build along high, narrow ledges of rock, and bridge wild mountain rivers. They often had to cut tunnels under or through mountains, and find passes through the big ranges.

Dr. Hector, an early explorer, had already found the Kicking Horse Pass through the Rocky Mountains. He called it that because while he and his party were standing at the meeting of two rivers, Dr. Hector's horse kicked him in the chest. He was badly hurt and his friends had to get him out as quickly as they could. They took the east-running river and it led them through a pass to the prairies. They named it the Kicking Horse Pass.

Next, Walter Moberly, a young British Columbian, discovered a pass through the Gold Range. Moberly and

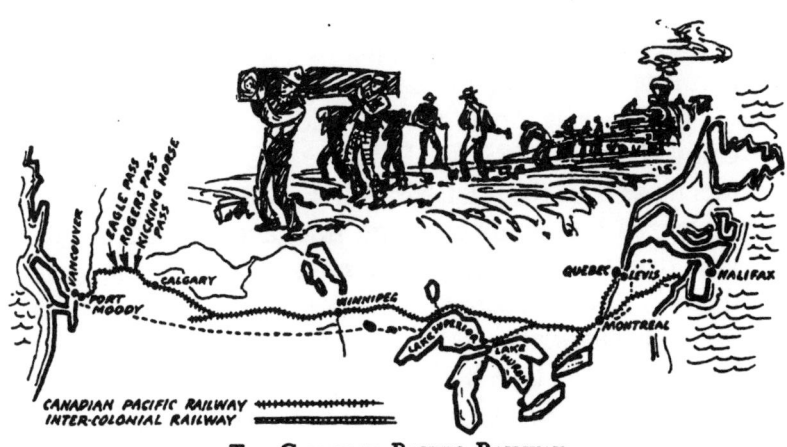

The Canadian Pacific Railway

141

his Indian guides had paddled across Shuswap Lake. While the Indians boiled the kettle, Moberly studied the Gold Range Mountains facing him. A creek tumbled down a valley beside the nearest mountain and two old eagles were circling over their nest feeding their nestlings. Moberly fired at them and they flew off up the creek.

"I wonder," thought Moberly, "if that creek would lead us through the Gold Range."

Moberly was not to be the one to find out. Winter was coming and his Indians refused to go farther. He was forced to return to Victoria. There he met Major Rogers and his nephew, Albert, who were exploring for Van Horne. They followed Moberly's creek up into the mountains. They had a terrible trip, but the creek led them through, so by the time the railway reached the Kicking Horse Pass, the builders knew the way through the Rogers and Eagle Passes, and on to the Pacific.

By this time, thousands of Chinese workmen were building the railway up from Port Moody, on the Pacific Coast, to meet the workers building through the Rogers Pass. At the same time, back in northern Ontario, 9000 men were dynamiting the rocks to get stone to fill the swamps and make a bed for the railway. It cost $500,000 a mile to build that part of the railroad.

But it was done in the end. One afternoon, at Craigellachie in the Eagle Pass, the builders from the east met those from the west. Sir William Van Horne, who had organized the building of the line, and Donald Smith, who had done most to get the money to pay for it, were there. A workman set the spike. Van Horne handed Smith the sledge hammer and he drove the last spike home. The longest railway then in the world was finished.

Soon the trains were bringing settlers from the east to

farms on the prairies, and six months later passenger trains were running regularly from Halifax to Port Moody, and on to little new Vancouver. Our 4000-mile-wide Canada was tied together.

# 17    The Provinces United to Make Our Canada
### 1850 to 1885

**1. The provinces were growing up.**

By this time the pioneers were getting to be old men and women. They had worked hard and made money at their farming, fishing, lumbering, and ship-buiding. They had long ago left their log cabins and built nice brick or stone houses. The men had cleared their farms and built good barns. The women had lace curtains and fine furniture in their parlours, and stoves instead of fireplaces for cooking and heating. The pioneers had built churches and schools, too. In those days the Government did not pay for schools, so the parents built them, and hired teachers to educate their children.

    Their children were now growing up, getting married, and taking over the farms. Now that the land was all cleared, one man could hardly work a large farm alone, and machines were invented to help him. Farmers now cut their hay with a mower, and their grain with a reaper. These machines cut the hay and grain, but did not gather it up. Daniel Massey, an Ontario farmer, opened a shop and made implements and machines for farmers. He and his son, Hart Massey, improved the reaper till they had built it into a binder that cut the grain, gathered it up, and tied it into sheaves. With the new machines farmers could work much bigger farms.

Most farms were now near a village that had a store, a church, a school, and a blacksmith's shop. The blacksmith repaired the farmers' machines and shod the horses that drew them. It was great fun to watch the blacksmith blow his bellows and make the flames shoot up. Boys and girls stopped after school to watch him shoe the horses.

Most towns now had a railway station as well as several stores, churches, an elementary and a high school, and often a mill or two. The towns were laid out in streets planted with trees, and the houses had narrow verandahs where the people sat on summer evenings. The towns on the sea-coast were doing well, too. Halifax and Saint John were busy ports with many ships coming and going in their harbours. Many of the ships were steamboats, which had recently taken over the freight business from the clippers.

AN EARLY NINETEENTH-CENTURY REAPER

145

Each province had a city. Quebec was the capital of Canada. The Governor-General lived there. The people of Quebec were very fashionable; they gave big dinners and grand parties. Toronto was already a large, handsome, well laid out city. The streets were wide and straight; it was the first Canadian city to have sidewalks. There were many good buildings and English visitors said that the stores were as fine as those in England. But most of the buildings were wooden and fires were common. There was no fire department, so if a building caught fire it usually burned down.

The roads were still not paved, but the law said that each man who lived beside a road must do a few days' work on it each year. That kept the roads up. The pioneers needed good roads, for in those days the stages carried the mail through the country. Britain owned Canada's post office. At first the ships brought the mail only to Halifax and Saint John and it was brought up through New Brunswick by road to Kingston. Later, Quebec and Montreal got their mail through New York and it went on to Toronto by stage. Each letter cost about twenty-five cents to send, which was a lot of money in those days; for that reason people did not write many letters.

## 2. The provinces all built schools and colleges.

It is important that every generation of children be given a good education. This happens at home, in church or in work places as well as in schools and colleges.

In those days many people wanted their boys and girls to learn more than they could teach them at home. The French Canadians did not build schools in their settlements. When they could afford it, they sent their boys and girls to the nuns' schools and the priests' colleges.

A PIONEER SCHOOL

The Loyalists and pioneers built schools in their settlements, but at first most of the settlers were poor, so their schools were just log shacks with a board along each inside wall for a desk, and benches for seats. The children used slates, and learned to read from the Bible. It was the only book they had. Women did not teach in those days and most men were working hard on their farms. So the teacher was usually a man who was old or lame, or partly blind, or not able to do farm work. Not many of them were good teachers, and the children did not learn as much as their parents wished.

When some of the pioneers grew richer, they sent their children to the private schools and colleges in their province. But some people now thought that all boys and girls should go to elementary school at least. Dr. Ryerson, a minister, was one of these. He went over to Britain to find out what they were doing there about educating their children. He thought the Scots' way was the best, so he came back and worked to get schools planned something like the Scottish ones.

The Government of each province divided it into school districts and made a law which said that the people in each district must build a school and pay a tax every year to keep it up. Also the law said that all children up to twelve years old must go to the school. At first the people who had no children were very angry about paying taxes to educate other people's children, but they got used to it and soon schools were being built everywhere. The provinces also built Normal Schools to train the teachers. Giving young people a better education helped Canada to grow up.

### 3. The Assemblies made the Governors and Council do what the people wanted.

You remember that the Loyalists insisted on electing their own men to an Assembly to tell the Governor and his Council what the people wanted done. But the Governors and their Councils would not always do what the Assembly men told them to do. Sometimes they made decisions by themselves without listening to the members of the Assembly. And sometimes these decisions were not good for the people.

But when the pioneers came, they would not put up with Governors who did not do what the people wanted them to do. They quarrelled with their Governors; in Quebec and Ontario they even fought against them. At last Britain sent out Lord Durham to try to stop the quarrel. Lord Durham played fair. He listened to the Governors' side of the quarrel; then he travelled round the provinces asking the people to tell him what they wanted.

In Ontario, Robert Baldwin told him that the people wanted the Governor in each province to choose men from the Assembly to make up his Council. These Assembly men had been elected by the people, so that they could tell the Governors what the people wanted. And Durham was to ask Britain to tell the Governors that they *must* do what they were told.

Lord Durham told Britain this, and after a while Britain said, "Let them try governing their provinces in that way." They tried it, and after a little practice it worked very well. This kind of government, where the men elected by the people say what is to be done, is the kind we have in Canada today. It is called *representative democracy*. The government is made up of a group of men and women who are elected to *represent* all the other people.

**4. Four of the provinces united to form the Dominion of Canada.**

Lord Durham said also that Ontario and Quebec should be united into one province. This was done, but it did not work well. The French and the English Canadians who, in the combined Assembly, were even in numbers, always voted against one another, so that no laws could be passed.

At last Georges Cartier, the leader of the French Canadians, suggested that they should divide into two

JOHN A. MACDONALD AND CANADA AT THE TIME OF CONFEDERATION

provinces again and have a Federal Government. A Federal Government is one in which each province elects a parliament to manage her own affairs, and also elects members to a united parliament to attend to business that concerns all the provinces, for example the post office.

While Ontario and Quebec were planning their federal parliament, they invited the Maritime provinces and Newfoundland to join them. Nova Scotia, New Brunswick, Prince Edward Island, and Newfoundland sent delegates to a meeting in Quebec, where a list was made of sixteen things about which each province should make her own laws, leaving all other business to be done by the Federal Government. In the end only Ontario, Quebec, Nova Scotia and New Brunswick agreed to join the union.

John A. Macdonald and the other leaders went to England to get the British parliament to pass a law uniting the four provinces. The parliament passed the law, Queen Victoria chose Ottawa as our capital city, and there, on July 1, 1867, our country was born. John A. Macdonald, whom the Queen had made *Sir* John A. Macdonald, was our first Prime Minister.

At first the leaders did not know what to call the new country. Should it be the "Kingdom" of Canada (like England) or the "Republic" of Canada (like our neighbour to the south)? Then Sir Leonard Tilley suggested "Dominion" which is a word used in Psalm 72 - "He shall have dominion from sea to sea." And so our country is called the Dominion of Canada and her motto is "From Sea to Sea".

Even with only four provinces, Canada was a pretty large country; she stretched from the Atlantic to the Great Lakes. But there was left all the wide west, from the Great Lakes to the Pacific and stretching north to

Hudson's Bay and the Arctic Ocean. Canada knew that if she did not take possession of the west quickly, the United States would do so. In the same year that Canada became a Dominion the government of the United States bought Alaska from the Russians; that meant that they owned the northwest corner of North America. Many Americans wanted their country to go from the Mexican border in the south all the way north to the Arctic Ocean.

At that very time the people of Red River were divided: some wanted to join Canada, others wanted to join the United States. That is our next story, and it is a very exciting one.

## 5. Red River made her choice.

The new Dominion of Canada hoped to take possession of the wide land north-west of the Great Lakes. She knew that the Americans were pouring into their own west and planning to move over and take Canada's too. Canada had a clever plan, but she had to move quickly and she made mistakes.

Canada was cut off from her west by a wild, rocky land north of the Great Lakes, and she did not know the western people. Red River was still the largest settlement. It was the centre for the Hudson's Bay Company families, and for the Metis fur traders and farmers. There were also in Red River a few Americans, and six Canadians who were rather boastful and not much liked. The Red River people were now quite near the American towns up the Red River. They went to them to trade, shop, visit, and to get their mail. The Americans visited and traded with the Red River people and were now trying to persuade them to join the United States.

Canada's plan was to buy the Hudson's Bay

Company's land and to appoint a Governor and Council to govern it. When the English settlers in Red River heard that Canada was going to govern them with a Governor and Council, and without an elected Assembly, they were bitterly disappointed. If they joined Canada, they wanted to be a province, with an elected Assembly like the other provinces.

When the Metis heard the news they were frightened, for they were told that Canada was sending men to take their farms from them. They did not like farming. Like their Indian grandfathers, they thought it undignified to work with their hands. Hand work was squaws' work. But settlers drive wild animals away; the Metis could no longer live by hunting. They had to farm to live.

Suddenly, some Canadian engineers arrived and began to survey (measure) their farms. When they saw this the Metis rushed to their leader, Louis Riel, and he went with them to order the surveyors off their land. Luckily the surveyors went away and there was no fighting, but Canada had made a bad mistake in planning to take possession of the west without talking and listening to the people who lived there.

The Metis were now sure that Canada meant to take their farms, and they planned to stand up for their property and to fight for their land. Instead, Riel persuaded the Metis, and the English settlers too, to elect a temporary Assembly and to make a list of their "rights", that is things they had a right to, such as the right to keep their farms and to elect their own Government. When the list was ready they planned to send it to Canada. Then, if she promised to give them their rights, they would join her.

While they were making their list of rights, Canada sent out Governor McDougall to rule Red River. But the

Metis wanted Canada to promise them their rights first, so they rode down to the boundary of the United States and kept McDougall from coming into the Red River country.

All this time the Americans in Red River had been telling the people not to trust Canada who had treated her so rudely, but to join the United States. The Americans said that the United States would let the Red River people form their own Government. A few of the English people and many of the Metis wanted to do this, but Riel stood firm for joining Canada and kept the Metis on Canada's side.

So far Riel had done well, but he now made *his* bad mistake. He put Thomas Scott, a young trouble-maker, in jail. When Scott made more trouble, Riel had him put on trial. He was found guilty and shot. Many Red River people were shocked, for they felt that the trial had not been a fair one. Many people who had supported Riel now turned away from him. Ontario, Scott's home province, demanded that Riel should be shot. Quebec defended Riel because he was partly French Canadian and the two provinces had a bitter quarrel.

DRIVING TO THE OPENING OF MANITOBA'S FIRST PARLIAMENT

Then Sir John Macdonald, who was still Canada's Prime Minister, did what he should have done in the beginning. He sent Bishop Taché and John Smith of the Hudson's Bay Company to ask Red River to send men to Ottawa to say what they wanted done. Red River sent men and they asked to have Red River made a province with an Assembly like the other provinces. Sir John promised that Canada would do that.

Red River was now happy and carrying on quietly till Canada should make her a province. But because of the shooting of Scott, many eastern Canadians thought Red River was the "Wild West", and they sent soldiers to keep order there. Many of the soldiers were from Ontario and they plotted to kill Riel for shooting Scott. When Riel heard this, he and his friends fled to the United States.

The next year Canada made Red River the Province of Manitoba and took her into the Dominion of Canada. She held her first election and, in March, her first parliament met. Red River had no Parliament Buildings, but her people took the largest house they had and worked for days to make it ready and to decorate it with flags and colourful streamers.

By ten o'clock that morning the roads were full of horses, carts, and wagons carrying the families to the opening of their parliament. When they heard the bugles, everyone pulled to the side of the road and cheered as they watched first the troops and then Governor Archibald in his gold-laced coat go by. Then as many as could followed him in to the Parliament House. The ladies were all dressed in their best, you may be sure, the white women in silks and satins; the squaws in their finery: Hudson's Bay blankets, feathers, beads, and war-paint. It was a lively scene and everyone was proud that Manitoba was a province of the Dominion of Canada.

LOUIS RIEL AND THE MÉTIS RISING

## 6. The Metis rebellion

The soldiers from the east did not catch Riel, but they treated the Metis who stayed in Red River very harshly. Most of them moved west to the Saskatchewan River. There they could still hunt for a living. But when the buffalo disappeared they had to begin farming again. They still disliked it and were not very good farmers, but they did try. Then, just as in Red River, Canada sent surveyors to survey their land on the Saskatchewan. The Metis were frantic. They wrote to the Government in Ottawa asking for the deeds (legal papers) to their farms. The agents on the Indian reserves wrote, but their letters were not answered. They sent men to explain to the Government, but nothing was done.

At last the Metis held a meeting. "We will have to rebel," they said. "That is the only way to get them to listen to us." So they sent for Riel, who was living across the boundary in Montana. He was now married and teaching school, but he came. He and the Metis held meetings and decided that they must rebel and fight for their rights. Perhaps *that* would make Canada listen to them. It did.

The Mounted Police had been watching the Metis, and now Superintendent Crozier telegraphed to Police headquarters in Regina. He said that the Metis were planning to rebel and that he was afraid the Indians would join them: that was the great danger. The Police might be able to hold the Metis in check, but if the native tribes rose against the tiny white settlements scattered across the prairies, the white people would probably all be killed.

Two tribes did join the Metis rebellion. Chief Big Bear of the South Cree brought his three hundred warriors to help Riel, and Poundmaker, the famous Chief of the Sioux, brought his.

Near the place where the North and South Saskatchewan Rivers meet, in Batoche, the small army of Metis rebels made their stand. Their headquarters was a little wooden church. The first battle was fought at Duck Lake where the Mounted Police were defeated. Further up-river a band of Indians killed settlers at Frog Lake. Things looked very bad for the whites.

Two things saved them: Crowfoot, Chief of the Blackfeet, and Chief of Chiefs, remained loyal to his friends the Mounted Police, and to the "Great Mother across the Big Water" (Queen Victoria), but he had a hard time holding his young men back. The second thing was the Canadian Pacific Railway. It was almost completed, and the Government of Canada was able to send an army of volunteers west by train.

After a few more battles the Metis forces were defeated. Riel and the other Metis leaders fled. Riel was captured and taken to Regina. Poundmaker surrendered. Big Bear was hunted for weeks and was at last found, starving. Riel, Big Bear, and seven other Indians who had killed settlers were tried and put to death. The others were

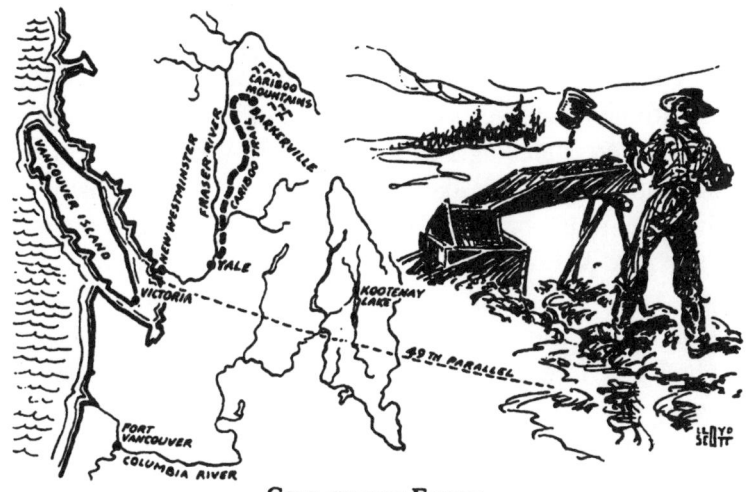

GOLD ON THE FRASER

pardoned. The Government in Ottawa now gave deeds for their lands to all the Metis. If it had done so in the beginning, there would probably never have been any Metis rising.

There was one good thing that came out of the Metis rebellion. The people in Eastern Canada now knew much more about the West; they were interested in it. After the fighting was over, many soldiers stayed on the prairies to homestead. West and East did not seem so far apart anymore.

## 7. Gold! Gold on the Fraser!

You remember how the Americans beat David Thompson to the mouth of the Columbia River and built a trading post there. Later, while the United States was fighting against Canada in the War of 1812, the American company could not send food to their traders on the Columbia River, so they sold their trading post to the Hudson's Bay men. Ever since that time, the Canadians had been exploring and trading in all the far west, south to California. They expected that all the land north of the Columbia River would belong to Britain. But Britain and the United States agreed that the 49th parallel would be the boundary from Lake Superior to the Pacific. That was disappointing, but the Hudson's Bay Company moved their post at Fort Vancouver north and made Victoria on Vancouver Island their trading centre. The traders had to build a new trail to bring the furs down the Fraser River. They had a very hard time, but in the end they found a way.

Then Britain made Vancouver Island a colony and appointed James Douglas to be its Governor. The Company built a good fort at Victoria and Douglas had an Assembly elected and a school built.

All was going well when suddenly an exciting cry rang down the river. "Gold!" it said. "Gold in the sand bars of the Fraser!" An Indian had discovered it; a trader had tested it. The story was true; there was gold on the Fraser! The cry reached California where the gold mines were giving out. It rang round the world, and the "rush" began. They rode, drove, walked; they came by ship, boat, even in canoes. Thousands came and a wild mob they were.

But Governor Douglas, Judge Begbie, and Judge O'Reilly managed them. Douglas and his Assembly made a law that every gold miner must buy a licence in Victora to dig for gold on the Fraser, and that he must obey British laws. Wildhorse in the Kootenay was one of the wildest of the gold camps. There were shootings and murders every few days till, one morning, Judge O'Reilly rode in and called the miners together.

"Boys," he said, "I am here to keep law and order. Those who don't want law and order can get out. For, boys, if there is shooting in Kootenay, there will be hanging in Kootenay." After that, if anyone wanted to shoot anyone else they stepped over the boundary line into the United States. And there was law and order in the Kootenay.

There were no farms and the Company posts could not feed the mob. Governor Douglas did his best to bring in food, but at first many of the miners were nearly starved. The crowd on the mainland kept growing, so Britain made the mainland opposite Vancouver Island the colony of British Columbia with Douglas as its Governor also. Britain then sent out a company of soldiers to keep order there. They built New Westminster to be the capital of the new colony; and built the Cariboo Road from Yale, 480 miles along the cliffs of the Fraser, to the Cariboo mines.

For by this time the gold miners were pushing up the Fraser into the Cariboo, where they found the creeks richer than the sand bars had been. One "claim" gave its owners $2000 a day for a year. On Williams Creek, four thousand miners were digging in one seven-mile strip of sand. Their food, brought in by stages over the terrible Cariboo Road, cost a fortune. People died or were killed, but still more came. One party drove and walked all the way from Canada across the prairies and the mountains to the mines.

After a few years, the miners found less gold; some began to drift away, but many stayed to take up land and farm or ranch. The colonies of British Columbia and Vancouver Island had just united and chosen Victoria for their capital, when the new Dominion of Canada invited them to join her. The people talked it over for some time. Like the people in Red River, some wanted to join the United States, but the majority favoured Canada. British Columbia sent men to Ottawa to say that they would join

159

the Dominion if she would build a railway to connect them with the eastern provinces. Sir John Macdonald promised that Canada would build the railway, and British Columbia became our sixth province. Prince Edward Island came in two years later, which made seven of us.

# 18 The Eastern Provinces Went Into New Industries
### 1850 to 1895

**1. Nova Scotia went into coal and steel.**

The three Maritime provinces went on fishing and farming as they had always done. But now that they had railways and fast steamers, they went into "Big Business" too. The new steamers and railways needed coal, and Cape Breton had rich coal mines, so Nova Scotia began coal mining.

Deep down, the coal mines ran out far under the sea. The miners wore little lamps in their caps to see their way along the tunnels. They took great care to prop up the walls of the tunnels with strong posts, so that they would not fall and bury the men at their work. But sometimes accidents did happen.

There are many stories of the brave deeds done by the miners to save each other when the rocks fell in, or if there was an explosion. One of the bravest is about young Dannie Robertson. Dannie was fourteen and he drove one of the ponies that hauled the trucks of coal from the miners to the cage that lifted it to the surface. An explosion shook the mine and Dannie found himself on his back in his truck with his coat blazing. He sprang out of the truck, burning his hands badly as he tore off his coat. The lights had all gone out, rocks were crashing down, and poison gas was beginning to seep in. Dannie ran for the cage, but stopped short when he heard a child crying. It was the little boy who opened the door for the trucks which carried the coal along the underground railway. The child was too frightened to run and was hiding under a seat. Dannie ran back, seized the boy, threw him over his shoulder, and ran with him to the cage which lifted them to the surface.

Nova Scotia had another exciting new business: she began making candy. Her ships took grain and wheat to the West Indies and brought back sugar. Those that sailed to Africa or South America brought back cocoa and chocolate, which are made from the beans (seeds) of the cocoa trees there. Sugar and chocolate make candy. Boys and girls liked candy in those days as much as you do, so two companies began making chocolates. Moir's made it in Halifax; and Ganong's made it in St. Stephens, New Brunswick. Grandfather Ganong invented the chocolate bar. Perhaps his grandchildren helped him think of that.

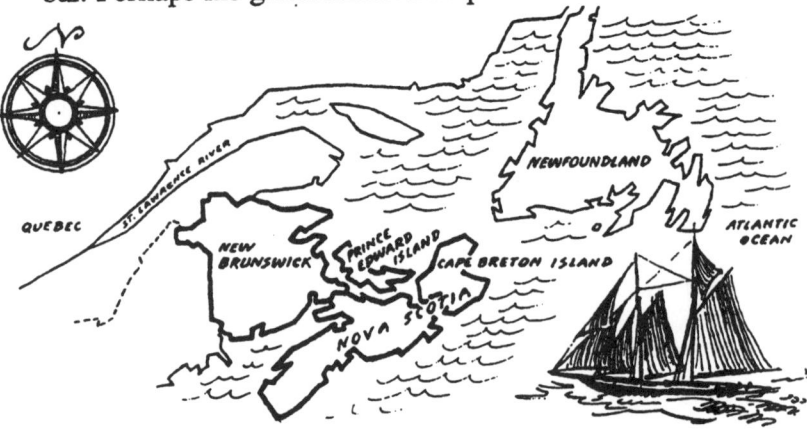

THE EASTERN PROVINCES AT THE END OF THE NINETEENTH CENTURY

## 2. Quebec led the way in mining.

The people of Three Rivers had been digging their bog-iron mine-field on the St. Maurice since La Verendrye's time. Their iron-works made cannon for the soldiers, and iron stoves and kettles which people were then beginning to use for heating and cooking.

While the people of Quebec were building a railway, they discovered asbestos in the mountains south of the St. Lawrence. Asbestos is made of long, silky fibres which will not burn. It is very useful for making fire-proof things. Canada has the largest beds of asbestos in the world. Nowadays asbestos is not used very much anymore because we know that asbestos dust can make people sick.

At about that time, too, Quebec miners discovered mica, a mineral which Hudson's Bay men had found long before on the shores of the Bay. Mica is transparent, like glass, but it is also tough, flexible, and a good insulator. For many years it was used in making electrical machines, but in your great, great grandfather's time it was used in making coal stoves.

AN EARLY COAL STOVE

In the evenings when the work was done and the family went into the sitting-room, father opened the draught in the tall round coal stove, and it made the coals glow and the little flames dance. The children could see the coals and the flames, for the middle part of the stove was made of little windows of mica, clear as glass. The family sat in the sitting room in rocking chairs, knitting or sewing, while someone read a story aloud, or played the organ and sang. If you were a child, you watched the red coals and the little flames dancing behind the mica, and ate Grandmother's cookies.

### 3. New Brunswick made new uses of her timber.

New Brunswick's big trees kept on growing. She had some bad forest fires, but millions of her great trees remained and millions of new ones began growing each year. And New Brunswickers found new ways to use them. When clipper ships went out of fashion, New Brunswick began building whalers, ships that went out to kill whales. Whales have thick layers of blubber (fat) under their skins, which was melted down to make oil.

PULP-LOGS IN NEW BRUNSWICK

The whale fishers told many good stories of their fights with whales. Mr. Seary tells an exciting tale in his book about the whaling ship *Margaret Rait*. She was sailing along in the Pacific, when the look-out man shouted, "There she blows!"

The sailors ran out the boats. The harpooners seized their harpoons and lances, jumped into the boats, and off they went after the whale. The mate's boat neared it first. He hurled his harpoon and hit the whale which turned like a flash, crushed the boat with its jaws and sank it. While another boat picked up the sailors, the Captain raced in to kill the whale with this sharp lance. But that whale just rolled over onto the Captain's boat and turned it upside down. The men got their boat righted and climbed in when, if you'll believe it, the whale came up under it and upset it again. Then, turning, it bit another boat in two! But while it was doing that, the mate got his boat near enough to drive his lance into the whale. That killed it.

New Brunswick's next new industry was pulp and paper making. Before this, paper had been made from rags. But rags were scarce and expensive. Then it was discovered that pulp made from spruce, balsam, and hemlock trees made cheaper paper. And there was New Brunswick with her forests of spruce, balsam, and hemlock, and her trained lumbermen and river drivers! The discovery gave her a very big new business. She built pulp mills at Bathurst and other places, and the river drivers began running millions of logs down to them. Sometimes the logs filled the rivers from bank to bank till you could not see the water.

A FOX FARM IN PRINCE EDWARD ISLAND

## 4. Prince Edward Island invented fox farming.

The island was "rocking on the waves" as she had always done. (Her Indian name, Abegewit, means "cradled on the waves".) She was still farming, all green and smiling. She had been specializing in growing potatoes and in shipping oysters and lobsters to the Boston market. Then, suddenly, she was the most exciting of all the provinces, for she invented a new industry. She began fox farming.

One year a Prince Edward Island farmer raised a few foxes on his farm. He got good prices for his home-grown furs, so other Island farmers began building fox cages and runs out of wire netting. Prices for wild furs were going up and more and more farmers began raising foxes. The silver fox has a very beautiful fur and the first twenty-five sold in London, England, for an average of $1,339 each. One beauty sold for $2,627. That was in the days when money was worth a lot more, too! The Islanders had their new industry

## 5. Newfoundland found an iron mine and built a railway.

Newfoundland was not yet a part of the Dominion of Canada, but it is important to follow her story during this time.

Towards the end of the last century it was discovered that she had a rich iron mine on Bell Island near St. John's. Now the Newfoundlanders had plenty of iron ore, and the Nova Scotians had plenty of coal, and with coal to treat the iron ore you can make steel. So the Nova Scotians built a big steel plant at New Glasgow, and began making steel. In this way the two neighbours helped each other.

The Newfoundlanders had been talking for years about building a railway. They all wanted one, but many of them said that they could not afford it. At last they appointed a committee to find out whether they could afford it or not.

The committee reported that they *must* build a railway. They said that there were now so many people living in Newfoundland that fishing alone would not support them. Newfoundland must begin farming, and keeping cattle, and should start other industries, as Nova Scotia had done. So money was borrowed and the railway was built and paid for. It opened up many more jobs for the Newfoundlanders. They found good farming land in the west, several new minerals, and a company built a big pulp and paper mill at Corner Brook.

## 6. Ontario had the first oil wells in Canada.

Oil wells had been found across Lake Erie in the United States, so Ontario searched for oil in the River St. Clair country and found wells that gave a thousand barrels a day. Well after well was drilled until they were getting two thousand barrels a day. A few of these wells flowed by themselves, but most of them had to be pumped. Now that people had oil, they gave up using candles and began to use oil lamps.

Ever since Brule and Jolliet had travelled across northern Ontario, Canadians had known that there was silver, copper, and gold there, but it was not until the Canadian Pacific Railway was being built that prospectors really began to explore that country. When they did, they found it rich also in nickel. Nickel was not much used then, but an engineer discovered that by mixing nickel and iron you get steel-nickel, a very hard metal. This discovery brought great wealth to Canada, for we have a great deal of iron, and the Sudbury nickel mines are the richest in the world.

The next find was cobalt. Hundreds of prospectors now flocked into northern Ontario. When they got there it was soon whispered round that some one had found gold. This was very exciting, and they all began tramping through the bush, searching for gold. Then one day a tired old man just jabbed his stake down where he stood and made the richest strike of them all, the famous Hollinger Gold Mine which became North America's largest.

# 19      The West Got New People
### 1870 to 1905

**1. First came the cowboys.**

While the eastern part of the prairies was becoming the Province of Manitoba, the western part was getting its first industry. Ranchers (cattlemen) were moving into the south-west. John and David McDougall had brought their cattle south from the Saskatchewan River and found that the prairie grass made good feed. It was green in spring, and under the hot summer sun it dried into good hay. Little snow fell in the south-west; the cattle pawed it away and fed out of doors all winter.

By this time ranching had spread from the southern United States into the northern states, and American cattlemen were beginning to move across the boundary into Canada where there was more and better grass. Canadian and English ranchers came, too. The Government in Ottawa rented each of them 200,000 acres of grazing land.

Each rancher looked over his land till he found a creek or a spring to water his cattle. There he built his ranch house, a bunkhouse for his cowboys, a sod stable, and a corral for the horses. Each spring the cattlemen held

169

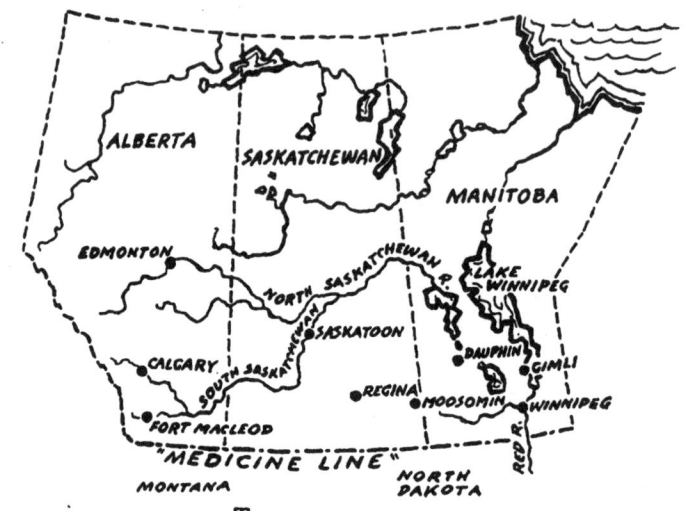

THE PRAIRIE PROVINCES

a round-up. The first Canadian round-up was held near Fort Macleod. It was a small one, for there were then only about a dozen ranches. The captain had only sixteen men in the round-up party and they had only one chuck wagon carrying food.

Later, the round-ups became very large with perhaps fifteen ranches each sending its outfit of chuck wagons, cooking and sleeping tents, cooks, and cowboys. Each cowboy had his own string of horses. The cowboys rode hard all day and had to change their horses often to keep them fit.

Everyone rose with the sun. While the cowboys breakfasted, the herders brought in their horses. Each man chose from his string the horses he wanted for the first ride of the day. The boys rode out in pairs, each pair rounding up the cattle from one part of the country. When all were in, each foreman cut out or separated the cattle with the brand of his ranch, and branded the new calves running with their mothers.

Each rancher had his own brand (mark), for example, TT (Double T). The brand was made with a small piece of iron in the shape of the mark. The calf was thrown

BRANDING A CALF

down and held; then the owner's brand was stamped upon the calf's side with the heated iron. It hurt, but not for long.

At the fall round-up, the cowboys cut out the cattle that were ready for market, and drove them to the nearest railway. Then they were loaded into cars and shipped east to be sold.

The Mounted Police now had a new kind of bad man to watch, the cattle smuggler. The Dominion Government had put a tax of $3 each on all American cattle brought across the boundary into Canada, and the police were ordered to collect it. Honest ranchers drove their new cattle up to the nearest police post and paid the tax. But the "Medicine Line" (the border in southern Alberta) is hundreds of miles long; the Police could not watch all of it all the time, so dishonest ranchers soon began running cattle across into Canada secretly.

One cattle smuggler crossed to Montana and bought five hundred cows, each with a calf. When he returned to the boundary, he ordered his cowboys to drive the cows straight to his ranch, while he drove the calves to the

Mounted Police post at Writing-on-Stone. There he paid the tax on the five hundred calves, and went home pleased with the way he had cheated the Government.

But the Police had been suspecting him. They hired cowboys to round up the smuggler's cattle, and found the five hundred cows with American brands on which he had paid no tax. The smuggler declared that he had not been smuggling and made a fearful fuss, but he paid the tax. After that, the Police watched him sharply. He got no more chances to be a cattle smuggler.

## 2. The homesteaders

While the ranchers were opening up the south-western prairies, the farmers were taking possession of Manitoba and the eastern prairies. The Dominion Government had given reserves to the Indians, and farmlands to the early settlers and the Metis. The Government now sent out surveyors to survey the rest of the west into farms for new settlers.

The surveyors laid out the land north of the boundary in townships six miles square. They divided each township into thirty-six sections of 640 acres, each with a 66-foot road around three sides of it as in the diagram. Then they subdivided each section into four quarter sections with 160 acres in each. You will see that each quarter section had a road down one or two of its sides. In those days, when farmers worked their land with horses, 160 acres was about as large a farm as one man could work.

Parliament then passed a law which said that anyone over twenty-one years old, or any head of a family, could have a quarter section free. He had to apply for it and send a $10 fee. When he had received his land, he had to build

PLAN OF A PRAIRIE TOWNSHIP

a house on it and live there, part-time, for three years, and plough at least 30 acres each year. This free land was his homestead.

It was a good offer, and many young men from eastern Canada came out west to take up homesteads. The railways ran special trains for them with cheaper fares. Tom Stewart and his friends, George and Mike Collins, came from Ontario on one. From Toronto to Winnipeg was a four-days' journey then, and there were no berths (sleeping compartments) and no diners on the train. The boys' mothers had packed big lunch baskets for them, but they were all tired, dirty and hungry when they reached Winnipeg.

Tom met his brother, Al, there and the next day they set out to choose their homesteads. They had quite a hunt, but in the end they found land near Moosomin. They applied for it, and paid their fees. Then they bought a pair of oxen, a plough, some tools, some groceries, and a pony and cart to carry their supplies out to their land.

It was the end of April, so they wasted no time but began "breaking" (ploughing) the very next day. Al led the oxen and Tom managed the plough. By the end of the month their money was almost gone, so Al went to work for a neighbour while Tom went on ploughing till they had forty acres ploughed to be seeded for the next year's crop.

It was now time to begin building their shack. As Al was still working to earn money for their winter supplies, Tom rode the pony to the nearest creek where he cut down trees and trimmed them into logs for their house. The oxen drew them home and Tom helped a neighbour to build his shack, and the neighbour, in his turn, helped Tom to build his.

By that time the wheat was ready to cut and all the bachelor homesteaders went to help the earlier settlers to cut and thresh it. When that was done, the bachelors closed up their shacks for the winter and went off to town to get jobs. Al worked as a carpenter in Moosomin, while Tom taught school not far off, and each saved his money carefully to buy tools, machinery, and cattle for their homestead.

### 3. Missionaries gave the Indians a written language.

All across Canada Christian missionaries lived and worked with the native people. They wanted the Indians to know about the God of the Bible. They taught them many other things, too. Some missionaries helped Indian bands begin to farm or taught them how to use new tools.

Some of these missionaries believed that it would best if the native people forgot their old ways and learned to live like the white settlers. They put many children into boarding schools where they learned English and weren't allowed to speak their own language.

But other missionaries lived with the native people and learned their language. You will remember Jean Brebeuf who preached to the Huron Indians and who was killed in an Iroquois raid. He learned the Huron language and even wrote a Christmas carol in Huron. Another missionary is remembered because he invented a way of writing these languages.

James Evans was living with the Cree Indians in northern Manitoba when he decided to create a written language so the native people could read the Bible for themselves in their own language.

English, our language, has an alphabet where letters stand for individual sounds. Because the Cree language is very different from English, Evans decided to make symbols that stand for syllables. He made fifty simple signs which he was able to teach to the natives. Then he built his own printing press out of an old Hudson's Bay Company fur-baling machine, used soot and fish-oil for ink, and began printing parts of the Bible.

Later other missionaries used Evans' system of writing for other native languages and for printing other books. This helped the Indians a great deal.

**4. New Canadians came from Europe.**

THE MENNONITES. Canada now offered homesteads to settlers from Europe. The first large group to come were the Mennonites. They are a religious people who wear plain clothes, work hard, and relax by visiting each other, and going to church. They are fine people, but they had been driven away from one country after another because they refused to fight in wars. At that time they were being driven out of Russia. They sent men to

Canada to see what it was like. The scouts reported that it was a good country. Our Government promised that they would never be required to fight, so they came.

In three years seven thousand Mennonites arrived. They settled on two large blocks of land on the Red River. They lived in villages in which each family had a lot with a house, barn, and garden. The people of each village built a church and a school, and elected a mayor and council to attend to the village business. They had no policeman. If anyone did wrong, the minister called a church meeting to decide how he or she should be punished.

The Mennonites managed so well that in a very few years they had paid back the money our Government had lent them for their journey here, and were improving their homes and roads, and sending their children to high school and college.

THE ICELANDERS. The next band of new settlers to come to western Canada were Icelanders. They were farmers and fishermen, so the first party settled on the west shore of Lake Winnipeg where they hoped to go on

NEW CANADIANS OF 1900: A MENNONITE, AN ICELANDER, AND A DOUKHOBOR

farming and fishing. They had brought with them their tools and twine to make nets, but they had not much money, so some of the young men and women took jobs in Winnipeg, and sent their wages home to their settlement. They called it Gimli.

It was fall when they arrived and they had not much time to build. A few of them got their houses up and they helped others build cabins and bank them with snow to make them warm. It was a long, cold winter and many were sick, but they had brought their books with them and they read the short, dark days away.

When spring came and they were spading up their ground, and getting their boats ready, eleven hundred more came. There was a happy meeting of old friends, and much excited talk as they exchanged news of the old home and the new. But smallpox broke out, and over a hundred of them died. Those were dreadful days, but when the sickness was over, they set to work bravely. They had a hard time, but kept on working to develop their settlement. Many sons and daughters of these energetic and hard-working Icelanders became leaders in western Canada.

THE DOUKHOBORS. The Doukhobors were the third large group to come to Canada. Like the Mennonites, they came from Russia. They were tall, strong people in sheepskin coats and big boots. They settled near Dauphin, Manitoba, where they worked hard and did well on their farms. Like the Mennonites, they did not think it was right to fight in wars, and Canada promised them that they need never join our army.

The Doukhobors believed that it is wrong to be educated. They could not read, or write, or speak English and, at first, they refused to learn. They would not build schools and, when the Government built them, they burned them down. Canada could not allow their children to grow up without being educated, and at first she had a good deal of trouble with the Doukhobors.

But by and by most of them gave in and began to obey the law. This group called themselves "Independent Doukhobors"; they moved away from the disobedient group and made new settlements, where they built schools, educated their children, and learned to live like other Canadians.

**5. Wheat made Canada world famous.**

Wheat was Canada's first grain and it is still her most important crop. Poutrincourt grew it in Port Royal. Champlain grew it in Quebec. The Loyalists and pioneers began shipping it to England, but it was Manitoba that made Canadian wheat world famous.

David Fife, an Ontario farmer, had some trouble with his seed wheat and he wrote to a friend in Scotland, asking him to get him some seed from the north of Europe. His friend sent him some, and Fife planted it, but

THRESHING WITH A STEAM ENGINE

only one seed sprouted. It sent up five heads. The cow ate two, but Mrs. Fife drove her away and saved the other three. They were planted, carefully watched, and replanted. In a few years David Fife had "Red Fife" wheat seed to sell.

Ontario farmers sowed more and more of it. Their bachelor sons carried it with them to their homesteads in Manitoba. It did well there. One year they sent a shipload to Glasgow, Scotland, to be ground into flour. The millers there were amazed. They found that Manitoba wheat was the "strongest" in the whole world. That means that when a woman uses Canadian flour to make her bread, buns, and cakes, they rise higher, and are lighter and fluffier than those made from any other flour.

The British millers called this new strong wheat "Manitoba" wheat. It was soon famous, and countries all over the world began buying it to mix it with their heavier wheats so that their women could make lighter bread and cakes.

Red Fife wheat made the strongest flour, but it had one fault. It took about 115 days after it was planted to grow and ripen. That meant that it was often caught by an early frost and was frozen. So Dr. William Saunders, the head of the Dominion Experimental Farm at Ottawa, began trying to grow a kind of wheat that would be as strong and good as Manitoba's, but which would ripen earlier. He and his son, Dr. Charles, kept mixing different kinds of wheat for fifteen years. By that time they had produced fifty-eight new kinds. They tested these to find out which made the best bread and cakes and ripened earliest. They decided on Marquis wheat, which ripens about 107 days after it is planted. This makes it pretty safe from the frost.

## 6. People kept on coming to Canada.

Many people had already come to Canada, and although they had moved into some of the empty places here, Canada still had thousands of acres of good farm land to offer to settlers. And Wilfrid Laurier, her new Prime Minister, planned to bring them here.

Laurier was a French Canadian. His family had come to Canada in Talon's time. His father was a farmer, a wise man who wanted his son to be educated in both French and English. Young Laurier was sent to school to a clever old Scot who made him read good stories and recite poems aloud till he could speak well in both languages. At college Laurier studied law. He was clever, tall, and handsome, and had charming manners. He seemed made to be a Prime Minister.

He was lucky, too. He was elected at a time when the world was enjoying good times; Canada had good crops; Britain was building more factories and needed our wheat to feed her workers. Everywhere, wheels were turning and people were moving. But Laurier knew that Canada needed more people, so he made Clifford Sifton minister in charge of settlement, and asked him to see what he could do.

Sifton advertised Canada's land in the United States' news-papers, and brought over trainloads of American farmers to see our land. Their west is much like ours, and they know how to farm prairie soil in dry years. In the next few years nearly a million Americans settled in Canada. Once he had made sure that the Americans were coming, Sifton turned to Britain and the rest of Europe. He advertised in those countries, sent immigration agents to tell new settlers how to come to Canada, and told the agents to book passages for them on the ships. Almost two million people came from Europe. They settled in all the provinces, but most of them came to the west. Several new railways were built across the prairies to carry the settlers to their land, and to carry their crops to the markets.

### 7. Alberta and Saskatchewan became provinces.

In early days, the prairies between Manitoba and the Rocky Mountains were called the Northwest Territories. They were governed from Regina, the capital of the Territories, by a Governor and a Council.

This Governor and Council were not elected by the people of the Territories; they were appointed by the Dominion Government in Ottawa. But Ottawa had promised that as soon as an area of one thousand square miles had one thousand settlers, the people would be allowed to elect a member to represent them on the Council.

After the railways were built, settlers came into the Territories rapidly, and by 1888 there were enough elected members in the Council to form an Assembly. At first, while the new Assembly made laws for the Territories, the Governor, who was appointed by Ottawa, still controlled the Assembly's money.

The prairie people did not like this. They wanted the Assembly they had elected to control the spending of their money. That is, they wanted a Responsible Government as the provinces of eastern Canada had. They kept on demanding this until, in 1897, Canada granted their request.

The prairies are so large that it was soon seen that they needed not one but two governments. So, in 1905, Canada divided the prairies into two provinces,

Saskatchewan and Alberta, each with its own government, sitting in their capital, Regina and Edmonton. The lands to the north were still called the Northwest Territories.

# 20  Canada in Three Wars
## 1900 to 1950

## 1. Canadians helped Britain in the Boer War.

At the end of the nineteenth century many people in Canada thought of themselves as Canadians as well as part of the British Empire. When English settlers in South Africa began to fight with the Dutch farmers or Boers, many Canadians (especially from Ontario) wanted to go there to help them. Other Canadians (mainly from Quebec) said that we shouldn't get involved in other people's problems.

Over 8,000 men volunteered and the Canadian government of Wilfrid Laurier paid their way to South Africa. This was the first time that Canadian soldiers fought in battles that were not in Canada.

## 2. After the First World War Canada became a nation.

While our provinces were building up their new industries, the different countries in Europe were building up theirs. The European countries are small and their

THE WESTERN FRONT ON 8 AUGUST, 1918

people are crowded together. For hundreds of years they had been fighting. Now, with their new industries, they became rivals in trade. For a long time Britain had been the richest and had had the biggest navy. Now Germany was rich. She built a big navy, trained a big army, and was ready to challenge Britain. She was just waiting for an excuse.

When a young man from Serbia shot the Archduke of Austria, it was as if a bomb had been dropped into a barrel of gunpowder. Everything blew up. Five nations called up their armies and marched them off to war. Britain tried to stop them, and held back her army till big Germany seized little Belgium. Then Britain went to war. Britain, France, Russia, and Italy fought against Germany and Austria.

When Britain went to war, the four Dominions, Canada, Australia, New Zealand, South Africa, and the British colonies of India and Ceylon (now called Sri Lanka), got ready to help her. They all thought that Germany meant to conquer and rule them. So they fought not only to help Britain, but for their own freedom. When

Canada called for soldiers, hundreds of our men volunteered to go to fight in Europe. In two months 34,000 young Canadians sailed to Britain to fight. Hundreds of Canadian women went too, to nurse the sick and wounded.

The armies fought many great battles. When the Germans were trying to break through our line to reach the sea, they attacked the town of Ypres where the Canadians were on guard. The Germans turned poison gas on our men there and many died in terrible pain. But those who lived held the line; the Germans could not break through. Later on, Canadians were sent to win back Vimy Ridge which the Germans had captured from the French. Three times the British and French had tried to recapture it and failed, but the Canadians won it and in the end they broke the German line and were the first army to march into beaten Germany.

This is only the Canadian part of the story. The men in the other armies, the British, French, Australians, New Zealanders, South Africans, the men from India, Ceylon, and other countries all had their brave fights and noble victories, too.

At the same time the war went on at sea and in the air. It was the first war in which planes were used. Planes were new then and, compared with the planes we have today, they were very poor ones. They were like big crates and had no modern safety devices. But our men were good at flying; several of them were "ace" flyers, that is, they shot down many enemy planes. Colonel ("Billy") Bishop shot down seventy-two enemies, the most destroyed by any one flyer on our side. For his bravery he was awarded the Victoria Cross.

Meantime the people at home had been working hard, too. The farmers grew extra crops; the town people worked longer hours; town boys and girls went out to help with the harvest. Women and girls knitted, sewed, and baked to send parcels over to the men. Sugar was rationed, which means that you couldn't buy as much as you wished. Many people saved money to buy war bonds to help the Government pay for the war.

The Dominions of Canada, Australia, New Zealand, and South Africa had over a million men fighting, and were spending millions of dollars on the war. So one day when their Prime Ministers were having a meeting, Premier Borden of Canada told Britain that these countries were not "colonies" any longer. He said that they were now grown-up, independent countries. They were earning their own living, and managing their own affairs.

"So," he said, "they should be called nations." Britain agreed to this. So the four Dominions became nations. They were still separate countries, but as they were all good friends they formed a society called the Commonwealth of Nations, so that they could work together.

At last, Germany and Austria were beaten. On November 11, 1918, Armistice Day, they surrendered. The news flashed round the world. People everywhere rushed into the streets laughing, crying, singing, and dancing for joy that the terrible killing was over at last.

## 3. Then came the boom.

The years after the war were very exciting. Canada had a boom; the whole world had a boom! A boom is a time when the farmers have good crops, all the factories are working, all the stores are busy. That means that all the people have jobs and are getting good wages. They have money to buy the things they want and everybody is happy.

Just before the war, and while it was going on, several new and exciting things had been invented: cars, moving pictures, radios, planes, trucks, new kinds of farm machinery. While the men were fighting, the factories had no time to make many of these new things, and those they did make all had to go to the armies. But as soon as the fighting stopped, the factories changed over from making guns to making the new machines.

At first the cars and radios and movies were very simple and crude; they would have made you laugh. But the factories improved them and the people bought them and enjoyed them. It was a wonderful boom.

**4. The bush pilots opened up the great northland.**

An important part of the boom was the opening of Canada's great northland by the "bush pilots". They were young Canadians who had been flying during the war. They loved flying and wanted to keep on doing it. There were no aviation companies in those days. The young flyers could not get jobs, so they made their own.

The scientists knew that there were minerals in the Canadian Shield, the wide band of rough land round Hudson Bay. Miners were working the gold, silver, nickel, and lead mines along the edges of the Shield in Ontario and Quebec, but no one had explored the Shield itself for minerals.

Then oil was discovered at Fort Norman. The Imperial Oil Company asked Gorman and Fullerton, two young flyers, to fly a geologist there to report on it. The young fellows leaped at the chance. Fullerton had engine trouble but got down with only a broken ski. Gorman got

A BUSH PILOT'S PLANE IN THE NORTHLAND

the geologist in, but smashed his landing gear setting down on the rough ice at Fort Simpson. When he tried to take off again, he broke his propellers.

Bill Hill, their mechanic, shook his head when he saw the damage, and Johnston, the mission carpenter, scratched his. But with boards held together with glue made from moose hooves, they repaired the planes. Then, with pilots, mechanics, and everyone in Fort Simpson holding their breath, the boys took off. Both planes flew. Fort Simpson breathed again.

After that, all the young pilots who could beg or borrow a plane, or who could stick one together, began to fly goods or passengers in and out of the northland. "Punch" Dickens made trips to Aklavik, where the Inuit took to the plane at once. The Indians and Inuit used planes regularly for business long before other Canadians. Dickens also made the first airmail flight, from Edmonton to Regina.

**5. When the boom burst.**

You know what a balloon looks like after it bursts, all shrunken and small. That is what Canada and other countries felt like when their boom burst. During the boom prices went up and up. In the end people could not buy any more cars, radios, machinery, and other things. So the factories had to close and the men lost their jobs. The weather was bad and the farmers had poor crops. They had little to sell, and no money to buy things. Many people would have starved. So the Government decided to help them by giving them "relief", that is, food and clothes or money to buy them. The hard times spread all over the world. It was a very bad depression.

The hard times were hardest on the high school boys and girls who were just ready to leave school and take jobs. Many older people still had jobs though they got very little pay, but there were no new jobs for the young people. The young men tramped round the country looking for something to do. Sometimes the trainmen let them ride in empty freight cars. The Government made labour camps for them where they built roads and did other useful jobs, but there was not nearly enough work for them all.

To make things worse, Saskatchewan had a dreadful drought. Summer after summer, for eight years, almost no rain fell and there was very little snow in winter. The grass died and the good top soil drifted off the fields, over the fences, and blew away in clouds.

In this great trouble Canada showed herself to be truly a nation. The people of the other provinces were poor themselves, but they all sent carloads of food and clothing to help Saskatchewan. The Government helped the farmers to dig ditches and build dams on their farms, and began building irrigation projects to use the rivers to water the thirsty soil. The scientists worked out ways of stopping the soil from drifting. They found ways of killing insect pests and preventing plant diseases. So the drought taught Canadians many useful things.

## 6. The Second World War

When the nations on our side had won the First World War, they all took their soldiers home and let them go back to work. They formed a society of nations called the League of Nations to guard the peace: But the League could only talk; it had no army to keep the countries from attacking one another.

Most people do not want to go to war. War means that many fine young men and women are killed. So countries, where the people elect their governments, do not go to war if they can help it; they try to settle their quarrels by having friendly talks. But there are still many countries in the world which are ruled by dictators. A dictator is a man who is not elected by the people, but who rules his country by force. That is, he has a big army and if people do not obey him he puts them into prison or shoots them.

The dictators just laughed at the League of Nations. The dictator of Japan attacked China. The League scolded Japan, but could not stop her. Dictator Mussolini of Italy seized little Abyssinia. The Emperor of Abyssinia begged the League to stop him, but it could not.

Next came Dictator Hitler of Germany. Hitler was a strange man. He dreamed of making Germany master of the world and wrote a book about it. The Germans read the book and crowded to hear and follow him. Hitler became the head of their Government and was called the Fuhrer (Leader). He became the head of the army, too, and gave the army all the latest weapons, big guns and planes. Instead of marching, his soldiers travelled in cars and on motor cycles. They seized Austria, Czechoslovakia, Poland, Denmark, Norway, Belgium, and Holland.

EUROPE BEFORE THE SECOND WORLD WAR

Britain had promised to help Poland, so when Hitler attacked her, Britain declared war on Germany. Then, when Hitler attacked Belgium and Holland, the British army tried to help them. The King of Belgium surrendered, but the British soldiers fought on as they fell back to the shore at Dunkirk. There they stood helpless while the big German guns and planes pounded them. Big ships could not sail close enough to the shore to take the men on board. But when the radio broadcast the news in England, almost everyone who had a boat raced across the Channel in it to bring the men home. The German planes pounded them, too, but they saved most of the British soldiers.

The soldiers were saved, but they had had to leave their guns behind and it took time to manufacture more. Meantime the British had to stand helpless while the Germans collected boats to attack England. But Sir Winston Churchill was now Prime Minister and his

191

THE LITTLE SHIPS LEAVE FOR DUNKIRK

stirring speeches made everyone brave. In the end Hitler sent planes instead of ships and the Battle of Britain was fought in the air.

The British air force was small, but quite a few Canadian air-men had arrived, and together they fought like lions. Often one British plane would fight two or three German planes, and send them flaming down, while the people stood watching in the streets and fields. Thousands of men, women and children were killed, and thousands of buildings were destroyed, but the British won. Hitler then turned on France and she surrendered.

Canadians were now hard at work growing food, making guns, and training airmen. Our sailors guarded the food ships that crossed the Atlantic to feed Britain. Our army helped to guard Britains's south-east coast. Our airmen fought beside hers. But some of our best flyers had to stay at home to train our young men and those from the other Dominions. They set up a huge training ground on the prairies. Canada's Air Training Plan turned out hundreds of brave air fighters.

The surrender of France roused the Americans. They still did not enter the war, but they began to lend ships and money to Britain, and many young Americans crossed into Canada to join the Canadian army and air force.

Then suddenly, in 1941, the Japanese bombed Pearl Harbor, the American naval base in Hawaii. This brought the Americans into the war on our side.

By 1943, the British and Americans had won the war in Africa, crossed to Italy, and were marching north in that country. The Canadians played a brave part in that fight, and they did another important job in France. Our armies were now ready to attack the Germans in France, where they had built very strong forts. The British planned a trial attack on Dieppe and the Canadians were chosen to make it. They made it, were beaten, and a great many were killed. But in the trial attack the planners learned many things about the German defences. The deaths of our men saved hundreds of lives on D-Day.

D-Day was the day on which our armies made their big attack on the Germans. With the information the Canadians had picked up at Dieppe, the planners were able to plan well. It was a hard fight, but our Canadian army drove the Germans out of Holland, and the other armies fought their way east across Germany till they met the Russians marching west to meet them. The Second World War was over.

## 7. The years after the war brought many new Canadians.

In the war many, many people lost their lives; many European cities were destroyed. Life in Britain, France, Germany, Italy and other countries was very hard. There wasn't enough food; people had to live in crowded houses and apartments; many were without jobs.

So a lot of Europeans decided to cross the Atlantic to make their home in North America. Many chose to come to Canada; most of them settled in the big cities of

Montreal, Toronto and Vancouver where there were more jobs.

With all these new people who were willing to work hard, Canada began to have another boom. Life was much better. Houses were being built, factories were making things, people were earning money and spending it on the goods that were made in Canada or imported from countries around the world.

Canada had had some very hard times, but she had grown stronger and was ready to face the second half of the twentieth century.

## 8. Newfoundland joined Canada.

All these years Newfoundland had carried on bravely by herself as a British colony. After years of discussion she had won from Britain the right to elect her own Government and to manage most of her own affairs. The First World War brought her good times, but in the Depression she had very hard times indeed.

The Second World War brought her great prosperity, for both Canada and the United States had to depend on Newfoundland. Look at the map of North America and you will see that Newfoundland stretches away out into the Atlantic. She is like a great battleship standing far out

A CONVOY SAILS FROM CANADA TO BRITAIN

to sea to protect both Canada and the United States. This was fortunate for both countries, for Newfoundland lent them the land they needed to build on the island great naval bases for their fleets. As you know, the Newfoundlanders have always been great sailors, and they proved this again in the war. The older people organized themselves into Home Guard units and Coastal Patrols to watch the narrow inlets and lonely shores for enemy raiders. Over eight thousand of Newfoundland's young men and women served with the British or Canadian army, navy or air force, and over five hundred of them gave their lives in the fight for freedom and democracy.

After the war, Newfoundland appointed a committee to study the advantages of joining Britain, Canada, or the United States. You can imagine how glad and proud Canada was when in 1949 a majority of Newfoundlanders decided to join us. So Newfoundland became our tenth province and Canada was complete from sea to sea.

# 21 Bringing Canada's Story Up to the Present
#### 1950 to now.

### 1. A mari usque ad mare

Canada's coat of arms is quite beautiful and impressive. Try to find out what all the symbols mean. The Latin inscription or motto means "From Sea to Sea". In chapter 17 you found out where those words came from.

CANADA TODAY

When Newfoundland became the tenth province in 1949, Canada truly was a nation from sea to sea. Some have said, from sea to sea to sea, for there are three oceans that surround our country.

Canada is a large country, stretching 5000 kilometres east-west and 4600 kilometres north-south. There are 250,000 kilometres of coast. There are mountain ranges and great plains; there are mighty rivers and large lakes. There is no place in the world like the vast Canadian Shield.

Canada is rich in farm land, timber, and minerals. The growing of crops is Canada's leading industry; she can grow most of the food she needs for herself, except such things as citrus fruits, tea, and coffee. Most of Canada's farms are "mixed" farms, which means that the farmer keeps cows or meat animals, and chickens, as well as growing grain.

Almost half of Canada's land is covered with forests, which supply her with all the wood and wood products (paper, for instance) she needs. More than sixty kinds of metals and minerals are mined in Canada; among these are iron ore, copper, petroleum, and natural gas.

Canada's population is small; there are fewer than 28 million Canadians scattered across our wide land. You will agree that this is a small number when you remember how big our land is, and think of the 250 million people who live in the United States, and the 56 million people who live in little Britain. But the number of Canadians is growing; every year thousands of people come from other countries to become new Canadians and to share our life here.

It is perhaps because Canada is large and rich and has such a small population that other countries are not afraid of her. They know that she will not attack them. Canada is a peace-loving nation. She works in the United Nations for peace, and she lives at peace with her neighbours. The big canal system called the St. Lawrence Seaway is a good example of how two different countries, in this case Canada and the United States, can work together on a project which is useful to them both. The air age in which we live has made our country the air cross-roads of the world, and Canada allows planes from all over the world to fly above her land and to use her airports so that they can get to where they are going quickly.

Canada is between two of the strongest nations in the world, the United States in the south, and Russia just on the other side of her Arctic Islands. Though the United States and Russia have not always been friendly to one another, Canada is at peace with both, for she knows that only in a peaceful world can men, women and children do their best work and lead really happy lives.

In 1996 Canada's coat of arms was changed slightly and these words were added: Desiderantes Meliorem Patriam which is Latin for "They desire a better country." This motto is meant to remind us that a country is a growing, changing thing, and that we must desire (and work) to make it better and better.

## 2. Canada belongs to two big societies.

THE COMMONWEALTH. The Commonwealth is a group of nations which were once colonies of Britain. To each of them Britain sent a Governor, and he chose councillors to help him govern the colony. Newfoundland was Britain's oldest colony, but she had a great many more. They were scattered all round the world and were called the British Empire.

After Britain took Canada from France, Canada became a British colony. Then, you remember, Canada told Britain that she wanted to elect her own Assembly and Council and govern herself. But she said she still wanted to belong to the British Empire. Britain let her do both these things. Canada elected her own government and was then called the Dominion of Canada.

When the other large colonies, Australia, New Zealand, and South Africa, heard this, they too wanted to elect their own governments and still belong to the Empire. Britain said they could, and they did. Now that they governed themselves, the four Dominions felt that they were grown up, so they called themselves the British Commonwealth. The smaller colonies went on being the British Empire.

After the Second World War, India was the first colony to become an independent nation; but she decided to remain as part of the British Commonwealth. One after

199

another most of the other colonies became independent countries. Many (but not all) are still members of the Commonwealth. A few of these countries still recognize Queen Elizabeth II of England as their queen. That is why the queen's head is shown on our coins and some stamps. The advantage of being a member of the Commonwealth is that the members help each other as much as they can. They have meetings and talk over their problems. They trade with each other. The older Dominions help the newer ones with their difficulties.

THE UNITED NATIONS. The League of Nations which the countries set up to keep the peace after the First World War failed. One of the reasons it failed was because it had no army to act as policeman. After the Second World War the winning countries set up another society, the United Nations, to try to keep the countries from going to war again. Canada helped to form the United Nations, and her leaders have worked hard in it. It has no army, either, so it could not keep China from attacking South Korea. But the member nations sent soldiers to help the South Koreans. They drove the North Koreans and Chinese back to their own countries and ended that war.

The next fight was over the Suez canal in Egypt. The Suez canal had been built by a Company which paid toll to Egypt. The canal is very important to Britain and France and the other countries because their oil tankers use it to bring oil from Arabia through the Mediterranean, instead of going the long way round South Africa.

Israel and Egypt had been fighting. Suddenly Egypt's dictator, Nasser, seized the canal. France and Britain sent men to take it back. Russia took Nasser's side. It looked like a Third World War and everybody trembled.

But the United Nations sent their head man, Mr.

Hammarskjold, to make peace, and ordered Britain and France to get out of Egypt. They obeyed, but Israel still threatened. Meantime Mr. Pearson, the Canadian leader in the United Nations, had persuaded the United Nations to get up an "emergency army", not to fight, but to stand between Egypt and Israel to keep them from fighting. This plan worked and Mr. Pearson was awarded the Nobel Prize for Peace for his efforts.

The United Nations is still involved in trying to keep peace around the world. Canadian soldiers and political leaders have played a great and important part in this.

### 3. Canada gets a flag and an anthem.

Every country has a flag that represents it. A flag is a visible symbol that people can look up to. When we see our flag flying on buildings or in parades we can feel proud about our country.

For many years Canada did not have her own flag. She used the Red Ensign which was really a British navy flag. Then in the sixties, the Government decided to give Canada her own flag. It was decided to use a simple design of two colours: a red maple leaf on a white background between two red bands.

"O Canada" was written in French not long after Canada became an independent country in 1867. Near the beginning of this century it was translated into English and was sung as one of many patriotic songs. Another one was "The Maple Leaf Forever".

At important occasions both "O Canada" and "God Save Our Gracious King" (or Queen) were sung. But it wasn't until 1980 that the Canadian Parliament passed a law making a new version of "O Canada" the official national anthem.

**4. Canada has a big birthday party.**

In 1967 Canada celebrated her first centennial. Many fine events took place across our country; many people spent their holidays travelling to places they had never before visited.

The most spectacular event was the World Exposition (Expo 67) in Montreal. Millions of people from across the country and around the world came to see the interesting exhibits.

Those years were a happy and proud time for Canada. Most people had jobs and could earn the money they needed to live a comfortable life. Canada was respected around the world as a peaceful nation; and she helped others get and keep peace.

Many people continued to come to Canada as a place to find a new home and to make a new beginning. Canada was known as a country with open doors and opportunities for a good life.

**5. Canada develops her natural and human resources.**

For most of Canada's history her natural resources were her greatest source of wealth. Furs, fish, timber, minerals, grain - these were the products the land and the sea provided. People had to find or grow these resources; they had to work hard to develop or harvest them. In this century another important natural resource has become important: water. Water is used for many things like irrigation and producing electrical power.

In the years after 1950 when most people were quite well off, they could spend more time on leisure and cultural activities. Canadian writers wrote books and Canadian publishers published them. Dance and theatre companies entertained audiences. People went to concert halls to listen to all kinds of music. Painters and sculptors displayed their work in art galleries and public places.

Television became a big part of most people's lives. More and more time was spent on recreation, leisure and entertainment.

**6. Problems and opportunities.**

Canada, like every other nation, has problems, too. We live in a large and rich land; it is easy for us to count our blessings. But people do not always use their resources wisely; people make mistakes; people can be envious and greedy. Sometimes it is hard to know what is the right and good thing to do.

Because Canada is so large, people in one part of the country don't always understand the people in another part. During the Depression, many people across the country were generous enough to help the poor farmers in Saskatchewan; people aren't always kind and generous.

The boom years of the twenties were followed by a crash and a hard depression; the boom of the fifties and sixties has disappeared more slowly - not like a balloon bursting but like a balloon leaking air. More and more people are out of work. The prices of things in the stores aren't going up that much, but people are having to pay more taxes to the governments.

In the good years the government spent a lot of money for big projects; they gave money to help Canadians develop their human resources to create Canadian culture. They spent too much money and now the country and many families are in debt. It is not healthy for anyone to be in debt because you cannot spend your money on things you need or want; you have to pay off your debt. So Canada is seeing some hard times.

Some people in our country think that they would be better off having their own country; they think they could make better decisions and live a better life.

In all these problems and difficulties every Canadian - every man or woman, every boy or girl, every native or immigrant, every leader or average citizen - has an opportunity to be understanding, honest, caring, and generous. We can try to understand the way other Canadians think and feel and how they live their lives. We can talk to each other honestly and truthfully. We can care about and for one another with compassion and generosity.

One important part of understanding is knowing the story of our country, how she came to be and how she grew and changed over the years. We must also be willing to admit our mistakes and work at setting things right. Above all we must believe that there is a right way for communities and nations to live and conduct their affairs just like there is a right way to live for individual people like you and me.

# QUESTIONS and ACTIVITIES

## Chapter 1 - The People in the Story

**Before you read**

1. Who were the first Canadians?
2. How did they get here?
3. What did they do for a living?
4. What did they live in?
5. What did they use for transportation?

**After you read**

1. On a map of Canada show where the different tribes of natives lived.
2. What are some of the words, customs, activities and inventions we have learned from the natives who lived here before us?
3. Draw a picture of the Glooscap story.
4. Find and read other native stories.
5. Read the story of how the Viking settlement at L'Anse aux Meadows in Newfoundland was discovered and what the archeologists found there.
6. Draw a picture of a Viking ship with the coast of Canada in the background.

## Chapter 2 - How America Was Discovered Again

**Before you read**

1. What was life like in Europe 500 years ago?
2. What shape is the Earth? How do you know?

3. Why did the explorers leave Europe?

**After you read**

1. On a balloon or a ball sketch the continents of the Old World: Europe, Asia and Africa; leave out the Americas and Antarctica. This is what sailors thought the world looked like. Trace a route from Western Europe to the east coast of Asia; this route is what Columbus, Cabot and other explorers were hoping to travel.
   Now draw in the great "obstacle" that was in the way: North and South America.
2. Read about the famous voyage of Marco Polo from Italy to China two hundred years before Columbus. What things did he bring back with him?
3. What were the things that the Europeans needed and wanted from other places?
4. On a map of the Atlantic Ocean draw the voyages of Columbus and Cabot.
5. Why did Cabot want to sail from England?
6. Learn about other explorers who sailed across the North Atlantic.
7. Begin a time line for Canada's history. (About 1000 A.D. to 2000 A.D.) Show when the Vikings and Cabot made their voyages. Continue adding important events as you read this book.

**Chapter 3 - How White Men Came to Live in Canada**

**Before you read**

1. Which part of Canada did the Europeans find first?
2. Who was there before them and how did they live?

3. What was Canada like then - the land, the weather, etc.?
4. From which parts of Europe did the people come?
5. What were they looking for? Did they find it? What else did they find?

**After you read**

1. On a map of Canada's east coast show Cartier's exploration routes.
2. What was Jacques Cartier looking for?
3. What trade did Cartier and his men start?
4. Choose a scene from the chapter to illustrate. (Some suggestions: Cartier taking possession of the land for France, Gilbert's great party, the terrible storm.)
5. Draw a series of pictures to illustrate Cartier's part of the story.
6. Find out more about fishing: how the fish were caught and preserved, how they were used back in Europe, etc.
7. Research the life of the native Canadians who lived along the St. Lawrence.
8. On a world map draw Drake's route.
9. Make a "compare and contrast" chart for several explorers: Columbus, Cabot, Cartier, Drake and perhaps others. Some categories: full name, country of birth, country that sponsored the exploration, dates, number of voyages, accomplishments, etc.

**Chapter 4 - At First Canada Was All French**

**Before you read**

1. Have you heard the names Champlain and Hudson?

What do you know about these people?
2. Why was Canada all French at first?
3. What is the meaning of the word "monopoly"?
4. Why were the people of Europe so interested in furs?
5. On a map of Canada find these places: Cupids in Newfoundland, Hudson Bay, Quebec, Lake Champlain.

**After you read**

1. On a map show Champlain's travels and the settlements he built.
2. Why did the settlement of Port Royal fail?
3. Choose one or more scenes from the chapter to illustrate.
4. Use your imagination to write or act out the scene when Hudson is forced to leave his ship.
5. What do you think was the "Great Sea" the Indians told Champlain about?
6. Do you think it was right for Champlain to get involved in the Indians' battles?
7. Find out more about the natives of Newfoundland, the Beothuks. Why is this a sad chapter in Canada's story?

**Chapter 5 - The Settlers Worked Hard to Get a Start**

**Before you read**

1. Look at the headings in this chapter and the illustrations.
2. Where did the settlers come from?
3. What was Champlain looking for? (Recall the last chapter.)
4. Where is Acadia?

5. Why would a church and a school be important to the settlers?
6. What does the title "Father" mean in the name Father Jogues?

**After you read**

1. On a map show Champlain's trip to the Hurons.
2. On a map of Eastern Canada show the places and routes where Champlain and his men went.
3. What was Nicholas Vignau's story? Why do you think he told it?
4. Samuel de Champlain has been called "The Father of Canada" or "The First Canadian". Why?
5. Write about the successes, failures and disappointments of Champlain.
6. Write a short story set at the annual Fur Fair. What kind of "problem" could make this an interesting story?
7. From the description in this chapter make an illustration of the Mission House which the priests built among the Hurons.
8. In your own words tell the story of Father Jogues. What would this story be like if one of the Mohawks were telling it?

**Chapter 6 - Both English and French Colonies Had to Fight for Their Lives**

**Before you read**

1. Where were the English and French colonies? Who had founded them? Why were they there?
2. Who were the enemies? Why were they fighting the colonists? Were people the only enemies?

3. Is it always easy to tell who are "the good guys" and "the bad guys"?
4. Did anything good come out of this hard time?

**After you read**

1. Look at the four questions above again. Have your answers changed at all?
2. Make a list of people who should be remembered for their bravery and accomplishments.
3. Of all the people mentioned in this chapter who was the greatest hero? Why?
4. Illustrate one of the stories.
5. Don't forget to add events to your time line of Canada's story.
6. Do you have any questions that this chapter doesn't answer?
7. Do a "What If?" activity. Imagine: What if Dollard had not intercepted the Iroquois attack? Or: What if Ville Marie had been wiped out by the flood? Can you think of any other "What If?" questions?

**Chapter 7 - Canada Began to Grow**

**Before you read**

1. Look at the dates in the last four chapter titles (4 to 7). Why do you think more things were happening during this century?
2. What was the main industry in Canada at this time?
3. In what way did Canada grow? What caused it to grow?

**After you read**

1. What did the Iroquois do in the Huron country?
2. Make a detailed time line of the life and work of Radisson and Groseilliers.
3. Why did the two men slip out at night on their second trip? What did the Governor do when they returned? Was this right? Why or why not?
4. If you're the kind of person who likes to draw, do illustrations about Radisson and Groseilliers.
5. Practise saying and spelling these two difficult names. (The English nicknamed them Radishes and Gooseberry. Can you see why?)
6. What if Radisson and Groseilliers had not gone to the English? How might Canada's story have gone differently?
7. Chart their travels on a map.
8. How did Talon set Canada on her feet?
9. What did the admirals do to the Newfoundlanders?

## Chapter 8 - Canada Spread North, West, and South

**Before you read**

1. How can a country "spread"? What does that mean?
2. How far did Canada spread or grow during these years?
3. How did Canada spread?
4. Why was it important that Canada was growing? Was everyone happy about this?

**After you read**

1. Who are the important people in this chapter of Canada's story?

211

2. Make a "compare and contrast" chart about Champlain, Talon and Frontenac. All three helped build Canada; how was their work different?
3. On a map show the spread of Canada. Show the routes of the explorers and mark important places.
4. What did the native people think about these voyages of exploration? How was this good for them? How was it bad for them?
5. Illustrate an important scene or two.
6. Make a "compare and contrast" chart about the explorers in this chapter: Jolliet, La Salle, Kelsey. One category should be: What were they looking for? Or why did they go exploring?

## Chapter 9 - The French Canadians Fought the Iroquois and the English for Canada

**Before you read**

1. Why do people fight? Why did the French Canadians fight with the Iroquois? Why did the French Canadians and the English fight each other?
2. How long ago was this? How did people fight in those days?
3. Do people nowadays still fight? Why? Have the reasons changed?

**After you read**

1. What is a seigneur? Is there anyone like that nowadays?
2. Show Pierre Le Moyne's travels on a map. What dangers and difficulties did he and his men meet on the way?

3. Illustrate the story of the attack on Moose Fort in a series of pictures.
4. Who were the "wasps"? Who was the "Rat"? Why were these names used?
5. Why is Madeleine of Vercheres still remembered today? Do you think she is a hero?
6. Write the story of Vercheres from the point of view of one of the Iroquois attackers. Or from the point of view of the lieutenant who arrived at the end of the story.

## Chapter 10 - Peace and War: Good Times and Hard Times

**Before you read**

1. What is the job of the government? Is it possible to have a country without a government? What was the government like in the English and French colonies in the 1700's?
2. Why did explorers keep going west? What were they looking for?
3. Who were the Acadians?

**After you read**

1. Make a list of the things the Canadians used; beside each write where they got it or how they made it.
2. Make a list of the different people in a French Canadian community and what each did.
3. What were the Verendryes looking for? Did they find it? What did they see? Can you draw a picture of what they found?
4. Why did La Verendrye's sons not keep on exploring when their father died?

5. On a map show the Verendryes' travels.
6. How did life become better and easier for the Newfoundlanders?
7. What did Governor Osborne do for the Newfoundlanders?
8. Who were the Acadians and what happened to them?
9. Why did the French and English start fighting again?
10. In the early years of the war the French Canadians were winning most of the battles. Why was this?
11. What happened to help the English? (Why are they also called the British?)
12. Illustrate part of the Battle of Quebec.
13. What if Montcalm and the French had won that battle?

## Chapter 11 - The French and the English Got On Well Together

### Before you read

1. How can people get on well just after they have been fighting each other?
2. How much of North America was explored by Europeans by this time?
3. Don't forget to continue your time line of Canada's story. 1759 was a very important year; make sure you mark that.

### After you read

1. How did the English and the French help each other?
2. What happened to the Acadians? Where did they settle?
3. Why was the fur trade so important to the colony?

4. On a map show Alexander Henry's travels.
5. Illustrate an exciting part of his story.
6. On a world map show Captain Cook's voyages.
7. Draw a picture of the things that Cook saw when he visited the Indians of the West Coast.
8. What important work did George Vancouver do?
9. Which other country was interested in this part of North America? Why?

## Chapter 12 - The United Empire Loyalists Came To Canada

**Before you read**

1. What was the British Empire? Who were the United Empire Loyalists? What does this name mean?
2. What happened in the English colonies along the Atlantic coast?
3. How was the American War for Independence important to Canada?

**After you read**

1. Why did the English colonies fight against Britain? Did all of them join in the fight? Why do you think some did not join in?
2. Who were the Loyalists? Why did they come to Canada? How did they arrive?
3. On a map show the movements of the Loyalists.
4. How did the coming of the Loyalists change Canada?
5. Illustrate a part of this story.
6. How did Governor Haldimand help the Loyalists in Quebec?

7. Why do you think the Loyalists changed the name Frontenac to Kingston?
8. How did the government in Canada change during this time?

## Chapter 13 - The Canadians Won the Relay Race to the Pacific Ocean

**Before you read**

1. What was this relay race and who was running in it?
2. Why did they want to get to the Pacific?
3. Look at a map of Canada. Where do you think this relay race was run? What was the route?

**After you read**

1. On the time line mark when the different stages of the relay race were run. On a map of Canada show the routes that were taken.
2. Who was the first European to see the prairies?
3. Who was the first European to see the Rocky Mountains?
4. Who explored the Saskatchewan River?
5. What did Peter Pond plan to do and why did he not do it?
6. Describe in your own words Mackenzie's two voyages of exploration. Which do you think was more important? Why?
7. Illustrate a scene from Simon Fraser's voyage.
8. Why did David Thompson lose his part of the relay? How did that change Canada's story?
9. Find out more about one of the explorers of this chapter. Write a short biography.

# Chapter 14 - Red River Was the First Settlement in Western Canada

## Before you read

1. Where is the Red River? In which direction does it flow?
2. Which Canadian city is near the Red River?
3. What were the two main fur trading companies at the beginning of the 1800's?
4. Did the fur companies want settlers to come to the Canadian West?
5. Who are the Metis?

## After you read

1. Who was Lord Selkirk and why did he buy land on the Red River?
2. Who were the settlers? Where did they come from? Why did they come?
3. Who were the Nor'Westers? Why did they dislike settlers?
4. How do the Metis come into the story?
5. What kind of man was Governor George Simpson? Do you think he was a good leader?
6. On a map of British Columbia and Washington show the important rivers and trading posts.
7. Why did the fur traders ship furs to Fort Vancouver? Mark the route on the map.
8. Why do you think the Shuswap Indians wanted to kill the white traders? How did the Chief trader stop their plan? Did he do the right thing?

## Chapter 15 - The Pioneers

### Before you read

1. What does the word "pioneer" mean?
2. What do you know about pioneers?
3. Are there still pioneers today?
4. Would you have liked to live in the time of the pioneers? Why or why not?

### After you read

1. List and describe four kinds of work that pioneers had to do.
2. What is a "bee"? Illustrate one or more kinds of bee.
3. What did the pioneers do for entertainment?
4. Describe the transportation (roads and vehicles) of the pioneers?
5. What two kinds of travel began during this time?
6. Describe and illustrate the new businesses that began during this time.
7. Why do you think that the author of this history did not include fishing as one of Canada's first industries?

## Chapter 16 - Bringing in the Prairies

### Before you read

1. What are the Prairies? What is another name for this part of Canada?
2. Which regions surround this part of Canada?
3. What is this region of Canada like? Do you know anyone who lives there? Do you live there yourself?
4. Who lived on the prairies?

**After you read**

1. Who lived on the prairies first? Who were the newcomers?
2. How did people travel at first?
3. What were some of the problems the people had?
4. Who came to keep order there? Where did they come from? Who sent them? Was everybody happy that they came?
5. In your own words tell the story of how the whiskey traders were stopped.
6. Name three of the forts that were built. Can you find their locations on a map? Draw one.
7. What was the "trouble" with Prairie Chicken Old Man?
8. Why was Sitting Bull important? Tell the story or illustrate it.
9. Why was the Canadian Pacific Railway built? Show the route on a map of Canada.
10. Who were some of the people involved with building the railroad? What did each of them do?

**Chapter 17 - The Provinces United to Make Our Canada**

**Before you read**

1. Canada and Canadians have been around for hundreds of years. Why do we say that Canada was "born" in 1867?
2. Why did the provinces want to unite? Did everyone want this to happen?
3. How were other countries (for example, the United States, Great Britain, France) "born"?

4. Do you know of any country that was born or started or made since you were born? (In other words, is there a country that is "younger" than you?)

**After you read**

1. What were some of the new things that were happening at this time? How was life changing?
2. Why was the blacksmith important? Illustrate his work.
3. What were some of the problems at this time?
4. How was school different back then?
5. What were the Assemblies? How did the people win the right to have Assemblies? How were people chosen to be in an Assembly?
6. Which provinces first united to form the nation of Canada?
7. Why did some of the other colonies not join right away? Why was Red River afraid to join?
8. When did other parts of Canada join? Why?
9. Write or tell the story of Louis Riel. How was he important in the story of Canada?
10. Who found gold in British Columbia? How did that change life there?
11. Who kept the gold seekers in order? How?
12. Why was British Columbia given that name? What does it mean?
13. Be sure to bring your time line up to date.

## Chapter 18 - The Eastern Provinces Went Into New Industries

**Before you read**

1. What does the word "industry" mean? Is there more than one meaning?
2. What are some of the natural resources of Canada? How can they be used?
3. Are new resources still being discovered? Are new industries started even now-a-days?
4. Why do people go into new industries?

**After you read**

1. Make a chart of the industries described in this chapter; beside each write which natural resources are used and in which province they were started.
2. Make an illustration showing some or all of these industries.
3. Dramatize (act out) the story of "The Escape from the Coal Mine".
4. How did Nova Scotia and Newfoundland work together?
5. Draw a picture of an oil well.
6. How did these industries help the people of Canada?
7. Which of these industries is the most interesting to you?
8. Which of these industries are still going on today? Why have some of them stopped?

## Chapter 19 - The West Got New People

**Before you read**

1. What is the "West"?
2. Where did the new people come from? Why did they come? How did they come?
3. Was their coming a good thing?

**After you read**

1. Illustrate the life and work on a western ranch.
2. What work did the homesteaders do?
3. Write or act out a story about cattle smuggling.
4. Name some of the countries from which the new settlers came. Find the countries on a map.
5. Find out how immigrants can become Canadians.
6. How did wheat make Canada world famous?
7. Who was Canada's Prime Minister during this time?
8. Who advertised Canada? How was this done? Did it work?
9. Why did so many American farmers move into Canada?
10. Draw a map of a prairie township.
11. Do you know someone whose ancestors came to Canada at this time? When did your ancestors come here?

## Chapter 20 - Canada in Three Wars

**Before you read**

1. What were these three wars?
2. How was Canada involved?

3. Do you know of someone who was in one of these wars?

**After you read**

1. Where did the Boer War happen? Who was fighting against whom? Why did Canadian soldiers go there?
2. What did Germany want to do in the First World War?
3. What event started the war?
4. Which countries helped Britain? Why?
5. What great battle did the Canadians win?
6. How did this war help Canada become a "nation"?
7. What society was formed to keep the peace?
8. What happened in Canada after the First World War?
9. Draw two pictures to illustrate the boom and the bust.
10. Talk to someone who lived through the Great Depression. What was life like for them?
11. Why did the Second World War start? Who was fighting whom?
12. How did Canadians in Canada help the war effort?
13. Why did the United States join in the war?
14. How was the war won? Who won the war?
15. Why did so many people want to come to Canada after the war? Do you know of anyone who came to Canada at this time?
16. When did Newfoundland join Canada? Why?
17. Put the events of this century on your time line.

## Chapter 21 - Bringing Canada's Story up to the Present

**Before you read**
1. Review the time line you have made showing the main events of Canada's story.

2. How do you and your family fit into Canada's story? When did your family become part of Canada?
3. What are the important events in Canada's story at this time?

**After you read**

1. Draw or label a map of Canada showing the provinces, the surrounding oceans, the main features (mountain ranges, large rivers, lakes).
2. What is the Commonwealth? Find out how this organization has changed during this century.
3. How many countries belong to the United Nations? Are there any countries that do not belong?
4. Where are the headquarters of the United Nations? What does this organization do for its member countries?
5. Draw or paint a picture showing Canada's flag; use your imagination to make this picture interesting.
6. Learn all the verses of O Canada.
7. Talk to someone who took part in Canada's centennial celebrations or who went to Expo 67. Find out what life in Canada was like then.
8. In the year 1997 a big event in Canada's story was remembered and celebrated. What was that?
9. In 1999 the map of Canada changed. What happened and why?
10. What are Canada's resources? Which ones are the most important? Which ones are being used a lot now?
11. What are some of the problems in Canada? What is being done to solve them?
12. What can you do to be a good Canadian citizen?
13. Finish your time line of Canada's story.

# INDEX

Acadia and Acadians 24-25, 34-35, 38-39, 54, 68, 80-83, 87-88
Alaska 93, 95, 112, 151
Alberta 104, 181-182
Algonkian (tribe) 44-45
American War of Independence 96
Annapolis 97-98
Arctic Ocean 110, 151, 197
Argall, Captain 34
Arkansas (tribe) 57
Assemblies 99, 102, 148-149, 152, 154, 158, 181, 199
Assiniboine (tribe) 62, 77, 105-106
Assiniboine River 52
Athabaska 107-109, 120
Athapaskan (tribe) 3
Atlantic Ocean 111, 129, 133, 150, 193-195, 197
Baldwin, Robert 148
Battles 27, 45, 65, 72, 83-85, 118, 156, 183, 185, 193
"Bees" (work parties) 126-127, 174
Beothuk (tribe) 28-29
Biarni 5
Biencourt 34-35
Big Bear (Chief) 156
Big Elk (Chief) 105
Bigot (Intendant) 84
Blackfoot (tribe) 3, 106-107, 135, 156
Blood (tribe) 135
Boom 186-189, 194, 203
Boundary 135-136, 139, 153, 155, 158-159, 169, 171-172
Bourgeoys, Marguerite 41
Bow (tribe) 77-78
Brebeuf, Jean de 35, 43, 175
British Columbia 22, 122, 140-143, 159-160
British Empire 96, 183-186, 199
British North America 103
Brule, Etienne 27-28, 33, 168
Buffalo (Bison) 62-63, 106, 110, 117, 128, 134-135, 155
Bush Pilots 187-188

Cabot, John 11-13
Canada 16, 82, 96, 103, 144, 146, 149-154, 156, 159-160, 167, 186, 189, 192-204
Canadian Pacific Railway (see Railway)
Canadian Shield 187, 197
Canals 129
Candy & Candy-making 8, 162
Captain of Militia 75, 86-87, 102
Carleton, Sir Guy 97-98, 103
Carrier (tribe) 112
Cartier, Georges 149
Cartier, Jacques 16-18, 23, 104
Celebrations 48, 80, 91, 106, 121-122, 126-127, 133, 146, 154
Ceremonies 3, 33, 55, 57, 59, 62, 92-93, 106, 119
Champlain Trail 90
Champlain, Samuel 23-28, 30, 32-33, 35, 104, 178
Charlottetown 88
Charnisay 38-39
Chatique (Chief) 107-108
Children 124-126, 132, 144-148, 162, 164, 186, 192
Chinese 142
Chipewyan (tribe) 90-91
Church 35, 42-44, 51, 74-75, 80-81, 86, 88, 98, 101, 119, 144-146, 156, 175-176
Coal 161
Colonies 38-45, 79, 80, 83, 96, 158-159, 184, 186, 194, 199-200
Columbia River 113-115, 157-158
Columbus, Christopher 9-11, 12-13
Commonwealth of Nations 186, 199-200
CONFLICT 6, 18, 25-27, 29, 30-31, 34-37, 38-45, 46-49, 52-54, 57-63, 64-73, 79, 81-85, 94-95, 96-97, 105, 108, 112, 114-115, 117-120, 123, 125, 138-140, 148-149, 151-159, 171-172, 175, 177-178, 183-185, 190-195, 199
Cook, James 92-94
Cornwallis (Governor) 80
Council 75, 102, 148, 152, 176, 181, 199
Coureurs de bois 52-53, 66-67

225

Cree (tribe)   3, 156, 175
Crowfoot (Chief)   156
Cumberland House (fort)   108, 113
Cupids   28
DAILY LIFE   1-3, 74-75, 86, 88, 105, 124-129, 135, 163-164
Dakota (tribe)   53
De Monts   24-25
Denonville (Governor)   64-68
Depression   189, 194, 203
DISCOVERY (see EXPLORATION)
Dollard   44-45, 47-48
Dominions   184-186, 192, 199
Douglas, James   122, 158-159
Doukhobors   177-178
Drake, Sir Francis   20-22
DuLuth, Daniel   52
Durham (Lord)   148-149
Edmonton   138, 182, 188
Elections (see Voting)
Evans, James   175
EXPLORATION and DISCOVERY   5-6, 9-13, 16-17, 27-28, 32-33, 52-53, 3, 76-78, 92-95, 115, 157, 168
Exports   6, 14-15, 94, 162, 178-179
Farming   25, 26, 28, 42, 47, 50-51, 53, 71-72, 74, 78, 81, 83, 86-88, 97, 99, 101, 116-119, 124-126, 128, 130, 143-145, 147, 151-152, 155, 157, 159, 161, 166-167, 172-180, 185-186, 189, 197
Federal Government   150, 154-157, 169, 171-172, 176-178, 181, 183, 201
Fife, David   178-179
Fishing   12, 14-16, 18-19, 23, 25, 28, 38, 53-54, 71, 79, 80, 83, 90, 93, 99, 144, 161, 166-167, 176-177, 202
Fishing Admirals   19, 53, 79
FOOD   8, 12, 16, 19, 25, 28-29, 30, 37, 38, 40-43, 45, 47, 50-51, 56-57, 67, 76, 79, 81-82, 84, 86, 88, 93, 95, 97, 99-100, 111-112, 116-117, 119, 121, 123, 125-129, 135, 137, 140, 159, 164, 170, 173, 179-180, 186, 189, 192-193, 197
Forestry (see Lumber)

Fort Albany   66
Fort Athabaska   108-109
Fort Brokenheart   60
Fort Calgary   138
Fort Charles   49
Fort Chipewyan   109-110
Fort Douglas   116, 119
Fort Frontenac   59, 66, 101
Fort George   113
Fort Gibraltar   116-118
Fort Kamloops   123
Fort La Reine   77
Fort Langley   122
Fort Macleod   139, 170
Fort Nelson   62-63
Fort Norman   187
Fort Paskoyac   78
Fort Rouge   77
Fort Rupert   65-66
Fort Simpson   188
Fort St. James   112, 122
Fort St. Pierre   77
Fort Vancouver   122-123, 158
Fort Walsh   134, 139
Fort Whoop-Up   136-138
Fort William   118
Forts   26, 28, 39, 41, 43-45, 65-67, 69, 71-73, 76-78, 80, 83, 91
Fox (tribe)   53
Fraser River   111-115, 122-123, 157-159
Fraser, Simon   112-115
Fredericton   98
French Shore   54
FRENCH-ENGLISH RELATIONS   18-19, 34, 49, 54, 64-66, 68-71, 81-85, 86-92, 96, 102, 149, 153, 180, 183,
Frontenac (Governor)   58-59, 64, 68-70
Fur Brigade   109
Furs   2, 16-17, 24-27, 33-35, 39, 42, 46-50, 52-53, 59-60, 62-63, 74-75, 76, 84, 89-94, 105-110, 115, 117, 119-120, 122-123, 130, 151, 158, 175, 202
Gilbert, Sir Humphrey   18-20, 28
Glooscap   4-5
Gold   157-159, 168, 187
GOVERNMENT (See also Federal Government)   75, 79, 80-81, 101-103, 118, 136, 140, 144,

147-160, 172, 181, 186, 189-190, 194, 199, 204
Governor or Governor-General 75, 101-103, 130, 146, 148, 152, 154, 158-159, 181, 199
Grain 162, 174, 178-181, 197, 202
Grant, Cuthbert 118
Great Lakes (also see each lake) 67, 150-151
Great Onontio 59
Groseilliers, Chouart 46-50, 104
Gulf of Mexico 57, 61
Guy, John 28-29
Habitants 75, 86
Haldimand (General) 86, 99
Halifax 80, 133, 143, 145-146, 162
Health and Sickness 18, 25, 37, 39-40, 51, 77-78, 84, 88, 97, 101, 123, 126, 176, 185
Henday, Anthony 104-107
Henry, Alexander 89-92, 107
Hochelaga 17
Hooper, Thomas 97, 99
Horse (tribe) 77
Horses 106, 113, 128, 130, 134-136, 140-141, 145, 154, 161, 169-170, 172-174,
Hospital 40-41
Hudson Bay 30-32, 48-50, 64-66, 105, 120, 122, 151
Hudson Bay 163, 187
Hudson River 30
Hudson's Bay Company 49-50, 52, 62-63, 64-66, 104-105, 108, 112-113, 116, 119-123, 135, 151-152, 154, 157-159, 163, 175
Hudson, Henry 30-32
Huron (tribe) 3, 27, 32-33, 35-36, 42-45, 46, 67-68, 175
Icelanders 176-177
Imports 79, 162, 194
Indian tribes 3
Indians (also see specific tribes) 1-6, 10, 16-18, 20, 22, 47, 52, 62-63, 64, 66-67, 78, 88-89, 90-95, 105, 108-109, 111, 113, 118-119, 122, 134-140, 142, 152, 156, 158, 172, 174-175, 188
INDUSTRY 14-16, 24-25, 33, 46-50, 52-54, 74, 76, 88-92, 94, 99, 105-109, 119-123, 130-133, 144-145, 161-168, 169-171, 179-180, 183, 186-189, 194, 197
Inuit (Eskimo) 3, 110, 188
Iroquois (confederacy) 27-28, 36, 40-45, 46-47, 53, 58-60, 64, 66-68, 71-73, 74, 76, 91, 100, 121, 175
Jogues 36-37
Johnson, Sir William 91, 100
Jolliet 56-58, 168
Judge 75, 79, 87, 158-159
Kelsey, Henry 61-63, 104-105, 113
Kingston 59, 101, 146
La Salle 58-61
La Tour, Claude & Charles 34-35, 38
La Tour, Lady 39
Lachine 58, 59, 68, 129
Lake Erie 67, 129, 168
Lake Huron 33, 46, 53, 104, 140
Lake Manitoba 78
Lake Michigan 47
Lake Nipissing 33
Lake Ontario 100, 129
Lake Superior 43, 49, 52, 77, 104, 129, 140, 158
Lake Winnipeg 77, 107, 118, 121, 176
LAND CLAIMS 10, 13, 17, 18-22, 23, 28, 34, 42, 54, 55-56, 92-95, 113-115, 151-152, 155-157
Laurier, Wilfrid 180, 183
Lawrence (Governor) 81
LAWS and RULES 48-49, 53, 79, 87, 99, 102, 119, 134-135, 139-140, 146-150, 158-159, 171-172, 176, 178, 181
Le Moyne, Pierre 64-65
League of Nations 190, 200
Leif Ericsson 5-6
Lolo (Chief) 123
Long Sault 44, 47
Loyalists 96-102, 128, 131, 147-148, 178
Lumber (Forestry) 131-132, 144, 164, 197-198, 202
Macdonald, John A. 140, 150, 154, 160
Macdonell (Governor) 117-118
Machines 35-36, 137, 144-145, 174-175, 185, 187-189
Mackenzie River 110

227

Mackenzie, Alexander 109-113
Mackinac 59-60, 89-92
Macleod (Colonel) 137-139
Madeleine of Vercheres 71-73
Magistrate (see Judge)
Maissonneuve 41, 43
Mance, Jeanne 41
Mandan (tribe) 77
Manitoba 104, 119, 154, 169, 172, 175-179, 181
Maquinna (Chief) 94
Maritime Provinces 131-133, 140, 150, 161-162, 164-167
Marquette 56-58
McDougall (Governor) 152-153
McDougall, James 112
Meares 94-95
Mennonites 175-176
Metis 118, 138, 151-157, 172
Miami (tribe) 53
Micmac (tribe) 3
Minerals 161-164, 167-168, 187, 197-198, 202
Mining 158-159, 161-163, 167, 187, 198
Missions & Missionaries 35-37, 39-43, 46, 52, 55, 174-175
Mississippi River 56-58, 61, 83
Moberley, Walter 141-142
Mohawk (tribe) 36-37, 100, 101
Money 46, 48-51, 58-60, 67, 96, 99, 124, 129-131, 133, 142, 144, 146-148, 159, 166-168, 171-174, 176-177, 181, 186-189, 192, 194, 200, 202, 204
Monopoly 24-25, 76
Montcalm (General) 84-85
Montreal 41, 43, 58-60, 71, 73, 78, 85, 86, 89, 92, 104, 109-110, 129-130, 146, 194, 202
Moose Fort 64-66
Mother Marie 40
Mountain Passes 141-142
Natural Resources 1, 2, 5-6, 7, 14, 20-21, 50, 92-93, 99, 117, 131, 134, 152, 155, 158-159, 161, 163-165, 167-169, 178, 180, 202-203
Naywatamee Poets (tribe) 63
New Brunswick 97-99, 146, 150, 162, 164--165
New England 49, 68-70, 87-88

New Westminster 159
Newfoundland 13, 22, 28-29, 38, 53-54, 78-79, 83, 102-103, 150, 167, 194-195, 197, 199
Niagara 91-92
Niagara (tribe) 91
Niagara Falls 59, 129
Nipigon 76
Nipissing (tribe) 32-33
Nootka 92-95
North West Company 109, 112-115, 116-120
North West Mounted Police 136-140, 156, 171-172
Northwest Territories 181-182
Norway House 121-122
Nova Scotia 24, 80-82, 88, 97-99, 102, 150, 161-162, 167
Oil 168, 187
Ojibwa (tribe) 3
Okanagan Trail 123
Ontario 46, 100-103, 117, 131, 140, 142, 144, 146, 148-150, 153-154, 168, 173, 178-179, 183, 187
Ottawa (city) 150, 154-155, 157, 159, 169, 179, 181
Ottawa River 32-33, 44, 46-47, 64
Pacific Ocean 76-78, 104, 109-115, 142, 150, 158, 165, 197
Parliament 150, 154, 172
PASSAGE through AMERICA 16-17, 23-24, 30-31, 92-95, 104, 111-115, 122
Peace 3, 23, 37, 54, 74, 78, 86, 91, 111, 186, 190, 193, 198, 200-202
Peace River 109-111
Peltrie, Madame de la 40
Perrot, Nicholas 52-53, 55
Phips, William 68-71
Piegan (tribe) 114
Pilot (dog) 43-44
Pioneers 124-129, 134, 144, 146-148, 178
Pirates 20-21, 26, 38
Pitt, William 84
Placentia Bay 54
Plains (see Prairies)
Plains of Abraham 84
Pond, Peter 107-109
Pontgrave 23-27
Pontiac (Chief) 90-91

Population 50-51, 53, 80-83, 87-88, 97-98, 116, 151, 158-159, 167, 169, 172, 175-177, 180-181, 193-194, 198, 202
Port Moody 142-143
Port Royal 24-25, 34, 38, 68, 178
Portage la Prairie 77
Post Office (and Mail) 146, 150-151, 188, 200
Potts, Jerry 138
Poundmaker (Chief) 156
Poutrincourt 25, 34, 178
Prairies 47, 61-63, 76-78, 134, 137, 140-141, 143, 156-157, 159, 169-170, 172, 180-182, 192
Prime Minister 140, 150, 154, 180, 186
Prince Edward Island 88, 97, 99, 102, 150, 160, 166
Prince Rupert 49
Provinces 102-103, 140, 144, 146-150, 152-154, 160, 181-182, 189, 195
Pulp & Paper 165, 167
Quebec 25-27, 35, 39-41, 43, 45, 48-49, 56, 68-70, 75, 76, 84-85, 86, 92, 99, 102, 129, 131, 133, 140, 146, 148-150, 153, 163, 178, 183, 187
R.C.M.P. (see North West Mounted Police)
Radisson, Pierre 46-50, 104
Railway 130, 140-143, 145, 156, 160, 161-163, 167-168, 171, 173
Ranching 159, 169-172
Red Crow (Chief) 138-139
Red River 116-119, 151-155, 159, 176
Regina 156, 181-182, 188
Representative Democracy 149
Richelieu River 89, 99-100, 130
Riel, Louis 152-156
Robertson, Colin 118
Rocky Mountain House 112
Rocky Mountains 78, 109-110, 112, 114, 141, 159, 181
Russia & Russians 112, 151, 175, 177, 198
Ryerson 147

Saint John 35, 38-39, 88, 98, 131, 145-146
Saint-Lusson 55
Salmon 111-112, 123
Saskatchewan 63, 104, 181-182, 189, 203
Saskatchewan River 62, 78, 105-107, 155-156, 169
Sault Ste. Marie 55, 90-91
Saunders, William & Charles 179
School 35, 40-41, 101, 119, 126, 144-148, 158, 174, 176-178, 180
Sea-mammals (Whales) 99, 164-165
Seigneur (Lord) 75
Selkirk, Lord 116-119
Semple, Robert (Governor) 118
Seneca (tribe) 66-67
SETTLEMENT or SETTLERS 6, 15, 23-27, 28, 34-35, 38-41, 50-51, 53-54, 55, 74-75, 80, 83, 88-89, 98-102, 113, 116-119, 124, 128, 131, 135-136, 142, 146-147, 151-152, 172, 175-178, 180-181, 193-194
Seven Oaks 118
SHELTER 1, 2, 15, 24, 26-27, 28, 34-35, 40-42, 74, 80, 88, 93, 96-99, 101, 116, 118-119, 126, 131, 134, 144, 169-170, 173-174, 176-177, 193-194
Ship-building 59, 93, 144
Shuswap (tribe) 123
Sickness (see Health)
Sifton, Clifford 180
Simpson, George 120-123
Sioux (tribe) 53, 139-140, 156
Sitting Bull (Chief) 139-140
Snake (tribe) 78
St. Charles River 69-70
St. John River 87-88
St. John's 79, 167
St. Lawrence River 17, 42, 54, 74, 85, 92, 99, 101, 130, 163, 198
Stadacona 17-18
Steamboats 129, 133, 145, 161
Tadoussac 23-24
Talon (Intendant) 50-51, 55-56, 58, 180
The Pas 105, 107
Thompson, David 113-115, 157

229

Three Rivers 33, 46, 48, 71, 76, 86, 163
Toronto 146, 173, 194
TRADE 8, 16-17, 23-27, 28-29, 33-35, 46-50, 89-92, 93-94, 105-109, 114-115, 116, 119-123, 151, 157-158, 200
Trade Goods 16-17, 28-29, 33, 47, 59, 76-77, 89-90, 92, 93-94, 107, 114, 154
Trading Posts 24, 26, 33, 35, 38, 64-66, 76-78, 83, 90, 94-95, 105, 108-109, 112-115, 116, 119, 121-123, 157-159
TRANSPORTATION 3, 6, 8-13, 17, 19, 21, 30, 33, 49, 79, 57-61, 64-66, 76-82, 84, 87-88, 89-90, 92-95, 97-101, 105-111, 113-115, 120-123, 124, 126, 128-133, 134-137, 140-143, 145-146, 154, 156, 158-160, 161-162, 164-165, 170-174, 176, 178-181, 187-193, 195, 198
Treachery 27, 29, 30-31, 32-33, 39, 60-61, 67-68, 91, 123
Treaties 54, 86, 119, 157
United Empire Loyalists (see Loyalists)
United Nations 198, 200-201
United States of America 96, 100, 112-115, 135136, 139-140, 151, 153-155, 157-159, 166, 168, 169, 171-172, 180, 192-195, 198
Van Horne, William 140-142
Vancouver 143, 194
Vancouver Island 92-95, 158-159
Vancouver, George 95
Verendrye (La), Pierre & Sons 76-78, 104-105, 116, 163
Victoria (city) 142, 158-159
Victoria (Queen) 150, 156
Vignau, Nicholas 32-33
Ville Marie 41
Vineland 6
Voting and Elections 102, 148-150, 152, 154, 158, 180-181, 190, 194-195
Voyageurs 64, 76-77, 89-90, 110-111, 118, 121
War 3, 18, 27, 54, 81-85, 90-91, 96, 100, 108, 116, 124, 131, 183-187, 190-195, 199-200
War of 1812 157
WATER 45, 101, 169, 203
WEATHER 16, 18, 21, 30, 40-41, 47, 60, 72, 84-85, 90, 95, 98, 101, 125, 128, 169, 176, 179-180, 189
Whiskey Traders 135-138
Wild Rice (tribe) 56
Winnipeg 77, 116, 119, 140, 173, 177
Wolfe (General) 84-85, 92
WORK 2, 6, 7, 13, 14-15, 22, 24, 26-27, 35, 40-45, 46-47, 50-51, 53, 74-75, 80-81, 93, 99-101, 116-117, 121-123, 124-128, 131-132, 140-142, 144-147, 152, 172-177, 186, 190, 192-194, 198, 202-204
World War I 183-187, 190, 194, 200
World War II 190-195, 199-200
Worldview 7, 9, 11, 129
York Factory 104-105, 116, 121

## Using the INDEX as a STUDY GUIDE

Through Canada's story run several important strands like coloured threads in a weaving. This index will help you explore some of these themes. Major "theme-entries" have been high-lighted LIKE THIS; but there are other minor themes as well, for example, "Farming" or "Provinces" or a particular place like "Montreal" or "Winnipeg".

You could make a study of one of the themes, for instance, CONFLICT. Asking good questions is an important part of studying something. You could ask: Who is involved in the conflict? Is it between individual people or between groups? What is the conflict about? Does the conflict get resolved? How? Are there traces of old conflicts left in our day?

In studying some of these major or minor themes you might want to look at other books to get more detailed information. You might, for example, want to learn more about TRANSPORTATION or the importance of WEATHER in Canada.

All the many native tribes mentioned in the book have been listed in the index. There is also a separate entry for "Indians" as such. These entries could be a good starting point for a project on our first people.

In reading *My First History of Canada*, in becoming familiar with the themes of our story, and in learning to ask good questions, you will be prepared to study Canadian history in greater detail and depth as time goes on.

Notes:
This index has been prepared to include both terms (words in the text) and concepts. For example, under "Farming" you will find references to homesteading, even though the word "farming" may not be mentioned. Similarly, eating and meals are indexed under "FOOD".

Not every personal and place name in the text will be found in the index. Many of the international references of the last two chapters relating to the wars of this century have not been indexed since they are only indirectly about Canada's story.